£1

CARE TO HELP

CARE
TO HELP

Freddy Bloom

John Clare Books

First published in Great Britain by John Clare Books,
106 Cheyne Walk, London, SW10 0JR

© Freddy Bloom 1980

ISBN 0 906549 14 0

362.4

Printed & bound in Great Britain by
A. Wheaton & Co. Ltd., Exeter

To Robert A. Wenzel

Contents

Care To Help

Many people would like to help the handicapped or disabled and their families but they do not know how. There is embarrassment and sometimes fear caused by ignorance. Often help is given but it is the wrong kind. This too is due to ignorance.

This book aims to replace ignorance with understanding. There is nothing mysterious or threatening about the disabled. They are ordinary people who have something wrong with them. They often, literally, need somebody to 'lend a hand'. It is trite to say we all need help sometimes, that we are all limited or disabled to a degree. Each of us is as strong as he or she may be. We can run as fast as we can run and others can run faster. We hear as much as we can hear and most dogs can hear better. We see what we can see and many animals have better sight. We accept our limitations as part of what is normal. We conform.

There is comfort in conforming and we are uneasy and often irrationally critical of those who do not meet our accepted standards. We are frightened because we are re-minded of our own vulnerability. At the same time, we are human beings and it is this awareness of vulnerability that brings out our sympathy and compassion. These may be among our most noble emotions.

I certainly have no intention of counting on our nobility or finer feelings. This is meant to be a practical book. We all live in our particular societies and are, whether we like it or not, dependent on each other. If we have to live together, we might as well make a good job of it—this is important whether we are labelled 'disabled' or not. When we are ignorant, we are stupid and when we are stupid, we make a mess of things. To do a job well, we must understand what we are doing and when we have done it often enough, we become so adept that little effort or conscious thought is needed. We do the right thing automatically. Here familiarity does not breed contempt but smooth efficiency and a better life for all of us.

That is what it is all about. Let's see if we can help, not in any organised way as members of some society or organisation but simply on a person to person basis.

Today there is no civilised country in the world that does not recognise its responsibilities to the disabled through legislation and the provision of services. These vary from place to place and from time to time. All leave plenty for the voluntary organisations to do and most of these organisations need many more good voluntary helpers. But that is not our concern here.

We are concentrating on the ordinary people we all meet in our daily lives, the people who, we know, have something wrong with them and who might find us useful one way or another.

Obviously, we do not have to do anything. There is no law that says we have to help. We can turn a blind eye and get on with our own business. That may be more sensible and generally more comfortable. If, however, we do feel like getting involved or even if we just cannot avoid involvement, we might as well know what it is all about.

CHAPTER TWO

'Them is People'

Some books begin with a statement that all the characters and situations depicted are fictional and that any resemblance to the living or dead is coincidental or accidental. None of the characters in this book is fictional. All are very real. They are usually undisguised but even if readers haven't met them in person they will not be strangers.

Eva is in her 80s and she lives alone in her tiny cottage surrounded by a clutter of the accumulated possessions of a lifetime. She has often tried to weed these out but memories are dear.

Once she was a nursing sister with the Queen Alexandra Nursing Service. She travelled all over the world and saw service in two wars. Once she was married and once she had a little boy. That was a long time ago. He is now a middle-aged business man in Canada with his own worries which overshadow care for his mother. He knows she is as well as can be expected and he sends her a small money order from time to time. He writes twice a year—at Christmas and for her birthday—if his wife reminds him.

Since her retirement from active nursing more than 20 years ago, Eva has put on a lot of weight. She has a weak heart and has had a minor stroke. Shopping is difficult for her. She does her own cooking and keeps her home spotlessly clean, working at her own rate and in her own time. Twice a week a Home Help comes. Old friends come too but they are 'old' friends and are dying off. Eva's biggest fear is that she may have to give up her cottage and her independence. She is still the woman she always was. She is also a disabled old lady

George is now in his 30s, married with one daughter. The family lives in a bungalow on the outskirts of an industrial town. George is a draughtsman and works at home.

C.T.H.—B

He was born in Glasgow and was always a bit of a hell raiser especially on a Saturday night after a drink or two. He still likes his pint of beer. He likes sport, was never outstanding at football but made his mark at water polo. He could be described as a man's man.

A few years ago, when the doctor confirmed that his wife was expecting a baby, they went out to celebrate and were both so excited that they forgot to take their door keys. On their return, George decided that the only way to get into the house was to climb a drain-pipe to an open bathroom window. It seemed a good idea at the time.

The drain-pipe gave way. George fell and broke his back. For some time, he was paralyzed from the neck down but gradually he has managed to get some strength and control back in his arms and hands. He is a draughtsman again and working at home. It is not quite the way it used to be but he knows that he is lucky and that he should not grumble. He grumbles like mad.

Winston never grumbles. Sometimes he loses his temper and cries but not very often. He is seven years old now and has a passion for pink ice cream. He can always recognise the colour. He is good on colours. Shapes are more difficult. His mother loves him very much and brings him ice cream almost every day. He is still very finicky about food. Sometimes she brings vanilla or chocolate instead of pink ice cream. He will eat it but does not enjoy it as much.

His mother came from Jamaica where she left two of her children. She felt she could do more for them if she got a job in an English hospital. Shortly after her arrival here, she caught German measles. It wasn't bad. Then she discovered she was pregnant and about six months later Winston was born. He has a severe hearing loss and cataracts in his eyes. There seems to be some brain damage, too. It is still hard to tell. In spite of all the help available through the National Health Service in this country, sometimes his mother wonders whether it might not be better to take Winston back to Jamaica where her mother and the rest of the family would look after him and accept him.

Katie's mother too had German measles during pregnancy. It was so mild that it was only on looking back later that she remembered the temperature and slight rash. That it might be Rubella (German measles) never entered her head. She had studied law and is a qualified solicitor. Her husband is a barrister. They have an attractive house in the country and a small flat in London. They have three children, two sloppy cocker spaniels and a couple of horses. Katie, the youngest child, is the same age as Winston. She is a pretty, dainty child and that helps. Her speech is very bad indeed, almost non-existent, though her family can understand some of the sounds she makes. Her brother and sister seem able to communicate with her quite easily which amazes their parents. They try very hard in every way but Katie often loses her temper when they cannot guess what she wants. She has had two operations on her eyes and seems to be seeing much better. They have employed two private teachers of the deaf and both reported progress. Even a little progress meant a great deal. It was well worth the money. The family is well off but their expenses are high. The family's friends and relations react to Katie in different ways. Some treat her almost as if she were one of the spaniels. Others make believe she is not there. Soon she may be going to a residential school in Shropshire.

Not far from where Katie lives, there is another solicitor. His name is Ken and he was blinded some years after the war when he was part of a bomb disposal unit. He was a regular soldier and had a reputation for courage and determination. He still has that reputation. Despite his blindness, he decided to become a solicitor and he did. He does most of the things sighted people do. Of course, none of this would have been possible without the constant help of his wife. It certainly has not been easy for Ken. It has been hard for her. You may know them.

It is unlikely that you know Henry. He and his mother do not go out much. They have few friends. They live in a small terraced house on the outskirts of Brighton. She is the widow of a postman. Her elder son has emigrated to Australia.

Henry is the apple of her eye, the core of her existence. He is a nice looking man in his late 20s. He speaks slowly and with little expression. Most of his time is spent with his stamp collection. He does most of the shopping and looks after the tiny garden. Sometimes he goes for walks. His mother has a tendency to go with him.

He was a bright boy at school with a gift for numbers and it had been decided that he would become a chartered accountant. He was 14 when he had his first fit. There was no reason for it. It just happened. The doctors diagnosed epilepsy but you did not have to be a doctor to recognise the symptoms. After the first one, he had fits fairly frequently. It embarrassed the teachers and the other boys and it was suggested that he go to a special school. He was given drugs to control the fits. They made him drowsy. His mother was torn between her natural ambitions for her son and her need to protect him. Henry knew what he wanted—desperately, but he lacked the energy to take prolonged definite steps towards any goal. He tried special courses and work opportunities but something always went wrong. Either he had fits or he took drugs to control them and then suffered from side effects. Gradually all ambitions died away. He and his mother settled into their quiet isolated lives. Neither complains. They do not bother their neighbours and their neighbours do not bother them.

Nancy suffers from epilepsy but hers is quite a different story. She has been luckier than Henry in many ways. The drugs that have been prescribed for her since her first childhood fits have not interfered too much with her career. It is true that she really wanted to be a teacher but recognised that her *grand mal* attacks were unsuitable for a classroom. She went into business instead but, after a couple of years, felt so unsatisfied that she started afresh, taking a university degree in education. Then she met a man called Bob. They got married and have three daughters. Nancy still has fits. They vary in frequency and intensity. She has been on all sorts of drugs which have controlled the fits to a greater or lesser extent. Some have had undesirable side effects. Her doctor has changed and adjusted prescriptions. Bob and the three girls live with Nancy and her disability. She means a lot to them and the epilepsy is part of her.

Jane and Tom were a most attractive couple. She was pretty with dark sparkling eyes and a soft Scottish brogue. He was a handsome Londoner with a successful business. His war career as a fighter pilot added distinction and glamour to his reputation. Both were deeply concerned in local politics. They had two enchanting little girls and life was good.

Then Tom found himself stumbling and losing his balance for no apparent reason. His eyes were not as good as they used to be. He had multiple sclerosis. For the next 20 years, Tom slowly deteriorated. He used sticks, then a frame and then a wheel-chair. Slowly his body packed up. His mind remained clear and his determination to master his disease never faltered. There were months, sometimes almost a year of remission but the enemy was relentless. The disability and the pain increased.

With Jane's help he ran the business as long as he could. Then she and the daughters took over. It was an impossible situation. He needed constant help. He had to be washed and lifted and he had been a big man. Though he lost weight and his body contracted, Jane was not strong enough to do all that was needed. Tom insisted on entering a nursing home where a trained staff could look after him and give Jane some respite. She visited him every day. Both were heart-broken and could not take the separation. Tom came home again and Jane looked after him with the help of visiting nurses. Two years ago Tom died. Jane feels that an essential part of her has been amputated.

Every summer for many years now a coach load of handi-capped children from the East End of London drives off for a day at the seaside—usually Margate or Southend. Kenny has been going for three years now. The first time his brother Fred came too. Fred had muscular dystrophy. Just before his fourteenth birthday, he developed pneumonia and died.

Kenny also has muscular dystrophy. He is in a wheel-chair and has been for the past six months. He has been fitted with a new corset and harness that helps him to sit up, for his spine has become weaker. The coach parties to the sea are his idea of real fun, much better than outings with his parents. He enjoys being with all the other kids. They make as much noise as they want, singing at the tops of their voices. Some of the lyrics are pretty bawdy but nobody minds.

On these outings, there are always about half a dozen able-bodied teenagers from the district who go along as helpers and friends. One of them is Halfer. His real name is Arthur but he is a Cockney and he is only pint sized so his nickname was inevitable.

The trip to the seaside is long and there is always a stop on the way to get petrol, buy ice creams and spend pennies. The coach stops. There is a flurry of activity as portable wheel-chairs are unfolded and boys and girls are lifted out or climb down under their own steam, using crutches, Zimmers or whatever support they need. It is a busy, boisterous and somewhat unusual sight.

A waitress at the wayside stop last year saw the spectacle in amazement, 'Ye gods!' she said, 'What have we got here? Just look at them.'

Halfer heard her, drew himself up to his full height and with impressive dignity informed her, 'Them is people!'

No need to say more.

CHAPTER THREE

You There

Mrs W is 84 years old. She is a cosy little lady with surprisingly alert, shiny brown eyes. her colouring, movements and entire bearing remind one of a sparrow.

On a recent late Saturday afternoon her daughter had arrived to find Mrs W sitting exhausted with her feet up, shoes off and hat still on her head. She had a thoroughly contented expression.

'Lovely to see you,' Mrs W said. 'I was just having a little rest. It's the Scouts you see.'

The confused daughter said she didn't see and Mrs W patiently explained.

For a number of years she had been sympathetically aware of the local Scout troop and of the special week when they did jobs for bobs or five pences or whatever inflation made it. They also, in their nice old-fashioned manner, had to do good deeds. Mrs W knew that taking old ladies across streets had always been a popular good deed. Old ladies were in short supply locally which was bad luck for all those lovely young Scouts. She felt that the least she could do was to make herself available, suitably attired and always suitably grateful, to be taken across streets.

Most of the day she had just stood and waited. When she spied boys in uniform, she would hover uncertainly at the kerb. Usually their eyes lit up joyously when they spotted her. Occasionally a boy would be absent-minded and almost miss her and she would have to draw attention to herself. She had been taken across streets at least a dozen times that afternoon, twice by the same Scouts, one of whom had not even recognised her. He was intent on his deed, not its object. Anyway, the boys had gained lots of merit and she felt an enormous sense of satisfaction at having helped them.

Now her feet were sore and she was tired. It had all been very worth-while.

Splendid lady!

Of course, helping her was no trouble at all. She was attractive and co-operative. It was easy to see what she needed and no great effort to provide the answer. Further-more, she was charmingly grateful and in no way provided a threat or embarrassment.

Mrs W might, however, have been one of those old ladies who mutter loudly to themselves. Usually their hair is all over the place, they are often dirty and their hats are not on straight. They are accepted as being a bit gaga but they still have to get across the street. Nobody knows how they will react to an offer of assistance. They might have been drink-ing and become aggressive. The easiest thing is to leave them alone. Probably they don't really want to cross the street anyway and, if they do, somebody else can take on the job.

It is far safer not to get involved. Involvement is always dangerous. This is plain common sense even if it does not help anybody. The old girl might get herself run over but that is her look out. It is her fault that she is in such a state in the first place.

Mrs W or any other old lady might be clean, sober but blind. In that case it is unlikely that, at her advanced age, she would be adventurous enough to be out on the street on her own. It is usually younger blind people who venture out by themselves with their white sticks or guide dogs. If they are seen waiting to cross the road, most sighted people do want to help. It is easy to sympathize with the blind. One need only close one's eyes to imagine what it must be like.

Yet there are reservations. Does one interfere? Is one's help really wanted? Should one take the arms of blind people or ask them to hold on? What about the dog? He is large and does not look too friendly. Perhaps he would resent inter-ference. Actually, there is no need for the blind to go out by themselves. Surely, there must always be somebody willing to accompany them and then they would not present a problem. Their independence is really rather selfish for it puts ordinary people in a dilemma. Oh well, it must be terrible to be blind. It's unbearable to think about it. So goes the convenient thought process.

Most adults are not Scouts. Good deeds are not issues with them; they can do them or leave them alone. The real trouble is that sometimes there is no choice. One cannot always avoid other people's troubles even if one has quite enough of one's own. This is an imposition.

The fascinating point is that other people's troubles are often a completely unacceptable imposition only if those troubles are outside one's own personal experience and knowledge. To explain, let us take epilepsy as an example.

If you are an ordinary person with no experience of the condition and the woman sitting next to you in a bus suddenly becomes rigid, falls to the floor, jerks violently, is unconscious, foams at the mouth, possibly becoming incontinent at the same time, this all adds up to a frightening and horrible experience—something to which you should not be subjected. Here is a nasty imposition.

If, however, your own brother has had epileptic fits ever since you can remember, then you will see the woman on the bus with very different eyes. You will not be frightened. You will be understanding, do what you can do and take it all in your stride. Actually, you will have a certain amount of satisfaction in recognising something familiar and being in control, perhaps of the whole situation, certainly of yourself.

Even in our sophisticated society, there is still fear of anything that is strange. This may be primeval but it is also understandable. What is strange is also unpredictable and may turn out to be to our disadvantage. That is a danger or a threat. There is more to it. In strange situations we are not sure of ourselves. We do not know exactly what to do and may easily make mistakes.

We are brought up to avoid making mistakes. We do not want to do things that are wrong for many reasons, not the least of which is that being wrong gains no admiration from those around us.

Nobody has ever been heard to say, 'Congratulations!

You have really made the wrong decision there. How brilliant you are.' At least not seriously.

From early childhood we learn that when we do the right thing, something that is clever or desirable, we are praised and rewarded, which is nice. When we do the wrong thing, something naughty or stupid, we are reprimanded and sometimes punished, which is not nice.

Most of our lives are devoted to avoiding what is unpleasant and going for what makes us feel good. This is natural and normal but, since we are all doing it, there must be conflict not only among ourselves but also within ourselves.

It does not take much imagination to realise that if we all followed our natural, self-indulgent inclinations, we would soon have a state or community that was ludicrous, destructive and self-defeating. For our own good, we learn to compromise right from the start.

Every baby wants to eat, sleep, burp, relieve himself, be warm and loved. He does not want the discomfort of tummy aches, sudden noises or jolts, cold, hunger or rejection. He makes his feelings known by crying, often long and loud.

The most important person in the baby's life is mother. She provides or does not provide everything that baby wants or does not want. She is all-powerful.

Sometimes when baby is thoroughly enjoying the food that mother is giving him, she stops and says he has had enough. He wants more and yells. Sometimes it works and sometimes it doesn't. It is her decision. Baby has no choice. He must accept it.

Babies soon learn that a smile greets a smile, that if they cry there may be comfort or there may be an angry face, scolding or even a slap. They learn to put up with a certain amount of hunger often because they become conditioned to eating at certain times. Experience has taught them that food is not far off. They may have learned to recognise the noises that mother makes when preparing food. This early basic learning not to cry the moment he thinks of the satisfaction of eating may be his first lesson in compromise which, in this context, is another word for self-discipline.

Famous psychiatrists, psychologists and philosophers have produced impressive jargon and whole vocabularies to explain their theories. Historians, sociologists, educationists, religionists, have carefully chosen their words to say what seemed important to them. They have written hundreds and thousands of books. If you simmer the whole lot down to their very essence 99 per cent are concerned with how human beings, individually or in groups, have dealt with disciplining their actions, emotions and thoughts. That is what history and fiction and everything else that mentions men and women is about. Big deal.

And so our baby learns to be potty trained and to eat according to the customs of his home. In our particular society we hope he learns to be clean, to read and write, say 'please' and 'thank you', respect other people's property, and later to earn money to buy the things that he wants. In adult life there are certain things he does publicly and certain things he does privately because he learns not to offend those around him for, in most ways, they have taken over the role of mother. They can punish or commend him.

He does not always like this arrangement. It interferes with what he naturally wants to do. Children hate their mothers sometimes. Mothers are a nuisance. They interfere. And mothers sometimes hate their children because they impose themselves and interfere with what mothers want. School and teachers are horrible when a boy or girl would rather be doing something else, but education is needed. The police interfere in all sorts of ways. They also offer protection. Everything has to be weighed up. There is compromise all the time. Ordinary people have to use self-discipline constantly and they don't always like it.

They know it is right, they know it is necessary, but they still object to it. Their natural emotions pull them one way and their common sense pulls them another way. The conflict is further complicated by what we call guilt.

Guilt is the uncomfortable awareness of doing what is

wrong. It acts as a necessary brake on bad behaviour, which is good. It can also be ugly and destructive.

Normally it is based on childhood experiences of being good and getting a reward, being bad and getting punished. That is a fine, simple, childish concept. As one grows up, one learns that sometimes a person is 'good' and there is no reward and sometimes a person is 'bad' and there is no punishment. Only children or the child-like complain that life is not fair. And, to some degree, nobody every grows up completely. Resentment at unfairness persists.

Apart from the social training which develops our sense of guilt, there are some things which are inherently bad and ugly and can be recognised as such. Cruelty, needless destruction, unnecessary violence are abhorrent in themselves. Those who participate often find the guilt too much to bear and then try to justify their actions with phoney cooked-up excuses.

Religions of every kind enter the picture as well. All religions have their special rules. Adherents with sincere faith try hard not to break those rules and feel truly guilty when they do. Many people, however, pay lip service to whatever religion they profess. When they break the rules, they may have an almost superstitious fear of what their transgression might evoke.

There is, therefore, the dilemma that man needs the constraints of his conscience but he must be freed from stupid irrational guilt. This is nothing more than a fear of the consequences if he displeases those about him, whether they be his parents, neighbours, teachers, police or colleagues. He must free himself from the need to conform to their standards. He must learn to think for himself and make his own decisions.

His decisions and consequent actions are based on more than self-gratification or fear. His mother or mother-figure will have cuddled him and fed him, bathed him and played with him. She will have made him feel good, safe and secure and he will love her for this. As he grows up, he will want to do things for her, not just to gain her approval but because he wants to show his love. He wants to look after her and make her feel good. In the same way, he will learn to love his father, brothers and sisters and grandparents, aunts and uncles. They are his people. He feels safe and happy with them and so he loves them. He will feel bad if any of them are in pain. He will want to help if they are in trouble. He learns sympathy, generosity, loyalty and compassion.

It all takes time. The very young child believes that his parents can do anything in the whole world. They know everything. They are his grown-ups and all grown-ups are powerful. It takes several years before he can really accept that there are things his parents cannot do, that they make mistakes, that they feel pain and are frightened. He may resent the fact that they are not as great as he thinks they ought to be. It takes many more years before he can accept that they are vulnerable too, like all human beings.

So there we have people: full of desire to get their own way, full of fear of the unknown, full of guilt, full of love, full of conflict, full of aggression and full of sympathy. Oh, we must not forget the sex drive which comes into the picture in no small way, too. What a fascinating mess we all are.

Now what, the reader may ask, has all this potted theorizing got to do with helping the disabled? Everything!

We are discussing human beings, those who want to help and those who need help. Fundamentally they are exactly the same. They are vulnerable, they are scared, they want to do what is right. Doing what is right sometimes interferes with what they really want to do. They would like things to be the way they think they ought to be and things don't always work out that way. Probably the able-bodied think about this less than the disabled do.

Disabilities generally can be accurately and objectively described. The effect that disabilities have upon individuals can rarely be predicted. One talks glibly about the able-bodied but usually we are wise enough not to try to define them. To the disabled man or woman everybody who can help him or her is able-bodied which, of course, might include the deaf, blind or legless.

One more point. The disabled rarely exist in isolation. They have parents, children, wives, husbands, neighbours. Those nearest and dearest are often more affected or handicapped than the actual patient. They need assistance, reassurance and support in their own right as well as for the sake of the patient. They, too, are human beings and must be respected as such.

Now then, let us get on with it.

CHAPTER FOUR

Spina Bifida and Hydrocephalus.

Since spina bifida is one of the commonest major abnormalities present at birth, it is surprising that it has not
acquired a less technical and more easily remembered name.
About 1,500 babies are born each year in Great Britain with
this defect of the spinal cord.

In spina bifida some of the spinal bones, which normally
protect and cover the delicate spinal cord, fail to develop
properly and the normal bony projection over the spine is
'bifid' or, in plain English, there is a cleft or rift. A Professor
Nicolas Tulp is credited with first using the term spina bifida
in about 1632. That is a long time ago.

Today we like to think that there is a greater social
awareness of the needs and rights of the disabled. We are
also aware that one cannot sell any product, whether it be a
detergent, chocolate bar or automobile without the right
name. To 'sell' the public a greater understanding of this
particular disability, it might be a good idea to give it a more
acceptable title.

The national society which deals with it is called the
Association for Spina Bifida and Hydrocephalus (ASBAH).
Many of the medical aspects which follow are taken from one
of their publications.

Several abnormal conditions are included in the term
spina bifida and they may occur at any point from the back
of the head (encephalocele) to the lowest end of the spine.

Two distinct types can be recognised. Firstly in spina
bifida 'occulta' there is only a small defect and seldom any
involvement of the nervous system. It shows as a fatty
swelling or tuft of hair on the back. In the second type called
spina bifida 'cystica' there is a more extensive defect in the
spine through which the spinal cord or its coverings, or both,

protrude. In the meningocele type of spina bifida 'cystica' the lump on the back, which is covered with skin, contains only cerebro-spinal fluid and the meninges which are the covering membranes of the spinal cord. The spinal cord is normal so that there is no neurological abnormality and hence no muscular weakness or loss of bladder control.

In the much more serious and much commoner type called myelomeningocele, with which we are mainly concerned, there is protrusion of both the nerve tissue and its coverings. The imperfectly formed spinal cord and nerve roots usually form part of the roof of this swelling or 'sac' and, because the skin is usually defective the area is exposed to injury and infection which may lead to meningitis or an increase in the paralysis or weakness of the legs.

The degree of paralysis varies with the size and situation of the defect and from one child to the other. Since the spinal cord and associated nerve roots are involved, there may also be a loss of sensation and a loss of sphincter control leading to dribbling or incontinence of urine and faeces. While this is acceptable in a baby wearing a nappy it becomes a source of distress and inconvenience in an older child and needs careful management by doctors, parents and teachers to lessen the likelihood of damage from infection and back pressure on the kidneys which may lead to high blood pressure

The onset of kidney failure may be slow but it is progressive and may be a very real threat to life as the child grows older. Because they have little or no feeling the children are unable to contract the bladder normally so that it may become over-distended. They do not get 'a message' to indicate the need to empty the bladder and so there is the danger that the small reservoir of urine remaining will become stagnant and infected. Doctors may advise manual expression of the urine from the bladder at regular intervals by placing one or both hands on the lower part of the abdomen below the navel and the application of increasingly firm pressure in a downward and backward direction. The mother will have been taught how to do this without causing pain and intelligent older children learn to do it for themselves. Others may need the help of the school nurse or welfare assistant—and the friendly neighbour who really wants to give mum a break by baby-sitting can learn the trick in no time.

This procedure, like the emptying of urine collecting bags, can be done before and after school and during break periods and so cause little interruption to lessons. Bladder expression may not be considered advisable for all children and urinary incontinence in many boys may be satisfactorily overcome by the use of a suitably designed urinal fitted over the penis.

Many girls present a more difficult problem. If incontinence pads and protective rubber pants do not prove to be a satisfactory solution a urinary diversion operation may be advised to bypass the bladder.

This will probably be suggested for both boys and girls if there is a danger of damage to the kidneys. Many surgeons prefer to wait until the girl is old enough to understand the full implications and ask for the operation herself. The operation involves separating a loop of small intestine, into which the ureters (collecting tubes from the kidney to the bladder) are implanted, and bringing it out onto the abdomen to form a projecting spout so that an appliance may be fitted over it to collect urine. This operation is only performed when it has been established that control of the bladder will not be achieved naturally. It is not without complications. The stoma or opening may become infected or need to be renewed. There may also be difficulty in fitting the bag, particularly to a sensitive skin. It is important to appreciate that it represents yet another 'assault' upon the body of an already handicapped child and one which may present a rather startling visual experience to those concerned with his care.

Satisfactory management of the bowel problem, in which the child may not appreciate that his rectum is full of faeces, will usually have been achieved before he attends school. However, 'accidents' may still occur as a result of an unsuitable diet, some unusual stress or anxiety, or in older children, from a failure to take the prescribed medicines or time for the daily evacuation. Soiling and the associated unpleasant odour is distressing to all concerned but a sympathetic approach will reap benefits in restoring self-confidence and overcoming the problem so that social acceptance is achieved.

Hydrocephalus (Greek hydro = water, cephale = head) is another important complication which may be present at birth or occur soon afterwards in over 80 per cent of the babies born with myelomeningocele. It is caused by an obstruction to the normal circulation of the cerebro-spinal fluid which is formed in the ventricles, or series of connecting spaces lying within the substance of the brain. This fluid is constantly in circulation under varying degrees of pressure and is absorbed on the surface of the brain. It is only when an excessive amount is present, or there is a blockage in the circulation, that pressure builds up and hydrocephalus develops. It should be remembered that hydrocephalus may occur without spina bifida—for example as a congenital defect or as a result of meningitis.

The hydrocephalus may persist only for a short time or it may lead to a rapid enlargement of the baby's head needing appropriate surgical treatment to prevent damage to the brain. A shunt system with a one way valve is inserted into the ventricle and the excess fluid under pressure is then diverted from the brain cavity, usually to the heart, by means of a narrow tube. This tube or catheter is led from the ventricle outside the skull beneath the skin, down behind the ear to the jugular vein and so to the heart where the fluid then circulates with the blood in the normal way.

This form of treatment was introduced in Great Britain in 1958 and there are now many different types of bypass valve. The treatment may, however, lead to difficulties and complications. The tubes may need to be lengthened as the child grows, the upper or lower tube may become disconnected and, more importantly, the shunt may become blocked either at the upper or lower end and need to be replaced urgently.

Any child with spina bifida who is unusually listless, apathetic, particularly inattentive or appears to have a raised temperature, may have a urinary tract infection. The effects of a blocked shunt are usually more dramatic with the development of severe headaches, drowsiness or vomiting. When shunt blockage is suspected the child should be taken to hospital as an emergency.

Many children with hydrocephalus have eye defects such as squints but any change or deterioration of vision may indicate raised pressure of the cerebro-spinal fluid and this needs medical investigation to prevent the very occasional development of permanent blindness.

The upper limbs and trunk usually appear to develop normally and such development will be encouraged by the physiotheraptist to achieve maximum mobility and independence in daily living. It will often be found, however, that these children are not as dexterous as children of comparable age and this will show in activities requiring fine co-ordination eg: handwriting, use of scissors or handiwork.

Sensation in the lower limbs will be impaired and skin ulceration is common and difficult to heal because of poor circulation. Care should be taken to protect pressure points such as heels or buttocks or where there may be pressure from calipers. These children are particularly vulnerable to burns and scalds from unguarded radiators, over-warm bath water and hot water bottles. Calipers may require repair, renewal or adjustment and the child may therefore attend school, or be involved in other activities without them. It is important to ensure that the child's legs are handled with care to avoid fractures and bruising.

It follows from all this, that there is an enormous range of effects from a cleft in the spinal cord. Some are minimal and others are gross. In the past most of the children who had the added complication of hydrocephalus died. With the success of the shunting operation, they now survive. Where there has been no hydrocephalus, the brain will probably be unaffected though the body may be badly crippled. Where there has been 'shunting', the brain may or may not be affected. Obviously the personality of any individual must be influenced by his physical condition. The degree or direction of that influence is impossible to predict or assess and will depend on dozens of factors of which the family background is usually one of the most important.

When you meet a child or an adult with spina bifida, you might be meeting anybody. You just do not know what to expect. Try not to have any preconceived ideas. Just have an understanding of the possible implications of the condition.

There are, however, certain generalisations that are worth bearing in mind. Many of the children are extremely chatty and friendly but they are usually more at home with adults than with their own age groups for the simple reason that they have more social experience of adults. Their experience of play with ordinary kids is limited. This applies to teenagers as well.

Incidentally, this is, on the whole, the big difference between most spina bifida children and Thalidomide boys and girls. The majority of the latter have been educated in ordinary schools where, often despite tremendous difficulties, they have usually eventually learned to be integrated. This is not often the case with those suffering from spina bifida. Incontinence for one thing, mitigates against it.

Again, because of all the special attention that SB demands, the role of the parents is more demanding, exhausting and total. This forms a strong bond but one that can be so close and tight that the parents no longer see the personality of the child and there may actually be little communication. The parents are sometimes too worn out to talk much.

It is not uncommon for the parents never to have discussed the disability and its implications with the child—even when the child is almost an adult. Inevitably many of the teenagers, despite their devotion, gratitude and dependence on their parents, also have a deep sense of resentment, but the more severe cases leave little room for rebellion. A friendly stranger may be a wonderfully useful outlet for some of these emotions which may fill to overflowing, the boys and girls and their parents. Just listen.

There is also much resentment and frustration because the disability is usually obvious and people see it and are then blinded to the positive work potential. Employment is a big problem. It is a big problem for all disabled people particularly those in wheel-chairs. Add incontinence and most employers just do not want to know. But incontinence can be dealt with; wheel-chairs can be accommodated; and anyway spina bifida does not necessarily imply either or both.

If you are the type of person who is interested in this sort of book and disabilities generally, then it is possible that when you come across somebody with spina bifida, you may know more about the condition and its consequences than he does. Fine. Keep it to yourself. He does not want to be met as a case to be discussed, but just as a person, as himself. Do yourself a favour and meet him as such.

CHAPTER FIVE

Thalidomide

Thalidomide is a drug that was prescribed frequently during the early 1960s as a tranquilliser. It seemed to be effective and have no side effects until the world was shocked by the births of hundreds of grievously damaged children in most of the civilised countries. It is only in 'civilised' countries that doctors will prescribe sedatives for tense and sleepless patients, including pregnant women.

As with Rubella (German measles) the severity of the effect upon the unborn child depended on the stage of the pregnancy when the drug was taken. Some Thalidomide children were minimally affected having, perhaps, a malformed hand or abnormal ear formations. Others were born without arms and/or legs. Some were brain damaged. Others deaf. There was a universal outcry of horror and the manufacturers of the drug were sued. Some of the law suits took years and all have not been settled yet. Compensation ran into millions of pounds.

All the Thalidomide children are now grown up. Some were so badly disabled that they could not possibly be integrated and educated in ordinary schools. They will have to be institutionalised all their lives. In Great Britain the majority, even those with gross physical deformaties, were, where possible, put in ordinary schools. There, undoubtedly, they were first seen as freaks but gradually the other children learned to accept them and they became friends and playmates. The Thalidomide boys and girls learned to adapt to ordinary life and ordinary standards and to make the most of whatever potential their bodies had.

Today the majority are capable of earning their own living and of looking after themselves as far as possible. Obviously if they are lacking arms and/or legs, they still have their limitations but they have become accustomed to these and they see themselves as ordinary people who happen to be short of a limb or two, which is what they are. That is the way they want to be accepted. They don't want pity. They just want to be accepted as human beings.

Each one in a way is a success story. The degree of success depended very much upon the parents and how much independence they allowed their children to have. It is easy to over-protect. Most of them have been marvellous. Very few have become professional martyrs who use their child's disability as an excuse for getting attention themselves. Some inevitably were not able to cope at all and the children were fostered or brought up 'in care'. Some of these children have a chip on their shoulders. To have had, for example, no arms and no parents is a lot to contend with, but it is amazing how much humour even these children show in their attitude towards themselves.

I must tell you about one young man who has very little in the way of legs and just one useful 'flipper' where normally an arm would be. He was in his wheel-chair smoking. A strange lady came up and told him it was a very bad habit. He looked at her in wide-eyed innocence and asked, 'Do you think it will harm me?' He enjoyed that.

Thalidomide children as a group were not more intelligent than other children but they have had to learn to use to the fullest every bit of intelligence that they might have. They have had to develop strength and courage and very thick hides. Remarks like 'Oh, they should not have been allowed to live.' or 'Why do they let them out?' are often made in front of them. Perfect strangers will go up to them and press money into their hands. The motives may have been pure kindness but what *do* these people think they are doing?

Courage and thick hides are needed, too, in their relationship with other disabled people. Practically all the Thalidomide victims have had some financial compensation. Other disabilities which may be just as severe but where no blame can be placed specifically and successfully, get no compensation. There is resentment.

In fact there is a good deal of resentment in the whole scene. The victims have had to come to terms with their conditions (what's the alternative?) but many still grumble openly about such a drug being put on the market at all and about their mothers having resorted to it. There is also guilt, no matter how irrational, in some of the parents, and a consequent resentment that they should have to feel guilty. This was not an 'act of God.' It was a terrible mistake and mistakes of this magnitude are hard to tolerate.

The Thalidomide boys and girls, men and women, can be seen as a special group. They mostly come from a social environment where mother would naturally go to a doctor and get a tranquilliser for her disquiet or discomfort. They have been brought up normally and they have been freed from the most basic financial worries. Some of these children were so badly damaged that there can never be a question of adequate compensation for them or their parents. All this is true but it is also in conflict with their most fundamental demand. Each one does not want to be identified as Thalidomide, disabled, legless. Each wants to be Mary, John, Elizabeth, Geoffrey, David—individuals to be accepted as such. Actually, whether they like it or not, they are pretty special.

CHAPTER SIX

Epilepsy

When one thinks that there are about a quarter of a million people suffering from epilepsy in this country, it is extraordinary that there should still be so much ignorance about it. In our schools, there are least 100,000 children suffering from it in one form or another and yet the majority of teachers do not know what it is all about.

Basically, having epilepsy means having fits. Doctors Desmond Pond and Eric Johnson have compiled a booklet* that gives a comprehensive description of the disease in simple language and all the following quotations are taken from it.

'There are various types of fit, but all are, in essence, an electrical explosion in the brain. The brain is made up of millions of nerve cells which act alone and in groups, as batteries of computers, programming each other according as they themselves are programmed by messages from each other and by and from the findings and sensations of the body. There is constant activity through these cells producing a flow of minute electrical impulses or waves. These tiny waves can be picked up by a machine called the electro-encephalograph, EEG, which magnifies and then records them on paper.

'The EEG is a valuable instrument in the investigation of epilepsy. But our interest at the moment is that it shows a fit as a sudden electrical impulse that can sometimes be seen to start from a particular point or focus in the brain and to spread from there over part or even the whole of the brain. This chain reaction produces the fit we see. It can be of

---

* *Epilepsy and Fits* by Dr Desmond Pond and Dr Eric H. Johnson. *A Family Doctor* booklet published by the British Medical Association.

several types and the classification of types is important in considering both the cause and the treatment of the condition.'

There are three main types: major, minor and psychomotor.

'The major fit is called the *grand mal* or general convulsion. The individual may or may not have some kind of warning that a fit is imminent, but typically, he suddenly falls to the ground unconscious, perhaps with a gasping cry. He holds his breath becoming red or dusky blue in the face. The body is rigid. In a short time, usually only seconds, the 'chronic' stage begins. This means there are spasmodic movements of the limbs and body. They may be very violent, literally throwing the victim about. After some minutes this passes and is followed by a stage of exhaustion which may vary from just a few seconds to several minutes or even hours. The victim may be confused for a time on waking or may be wide awake immediately and able to walk away as though nothing had happened. During the fit, saliva will dribble from the mouth, perhaps in the form of bubbles giving the harmless but well-known stage of 'foaming at the mouth'. If the tongue is bitten, the spittle will be blood stained. This is often a frightening but not serious complication. Sometimes the sufferer will pass urine, and occasionally, faeces.

'Even a severe fit is rarely dangerous to the sufferer and he will soon be normal once more and able to carry on with his usual occupation. One serious complication must be mentioned, however, called "status epiliepticus", which merely means that the fits recur one after the other at so rapid a rate that clear consciousness is not regained before another fit starts. This condition is rare but can endanger the patient's life and should status epilepticus develop, it is wise for the person to be admitted urgently to hospital.'

Most people have at some time or another had an electric shock from a live wire on a lamp or iron. The severity of the shock depended on the voltage. If one remembers one's own reaction, the thought of an epileptic fit is more understandable. The brain is suffering from an electric shock.

Some people are more susceptible to these shocks than others. All sorts of things can set off a sudden electrical discharge through the brain cells. Some people have more resistance than others, but given a strong enough stimulus could have an epileptic fit. Babies have little resistance and so convulsions are produced in some of them by stimuli, such as a sudden fever, which would be insufficient in later life. Normally resistance strengthens as the child gets older.

'The second type of fit is the minor one, often called *petit mal*. It is most commonly seen in children and consists of a sudden short loss of consciousness lasting only a second or two. It is often described as an "absence". The child does not fall and there is no abnormal muscle movement. The victim may be unaware at first that anything has happened and will only learn that he has had an attack when he realises that the world around him has moved on a little without him. These minor turns may occur many times a day, but they appear to have little or no effect on the sufferer except that caused by the time lapse. If, for example, a child has a number of minor fits during class, he will miss some of what his teacher is saying and may even lose the general gist of the lesson.

'Another variation of minor fits is called a myoclonic jerk. This is a sudden spasmodic jerky movement of the limb. If it occurs in the trunk muscles, it may cause the body to bend suddenly, bringing the person to the floor. This may be seen in young children, or occasionally, with minor and major fits, at any stage.

'The third main type of fit is called "psychomotor". These start in a part of the brain behind the temple. The attack is a local one at first but may spread rapidly through the brain to produce a generalised fit. Because it arises in this part of the brain, there is sometimes a definite sign at the beginning of the fit that is always, or nearly always, repeated. This may be a sensation or "aura" that tells the individual that he is about to have a fit.

'It may be a smell, a pain, a particular thought picture, or a sudden gripping fear. On the other hand, there may be a particular movement at the beginning of the fit, visible to the onlooker but unknown to the sufferer, such as turning the head to one side, a movement of a limb, or just a turning of one or both eyes. If parents or relatives notice that any such movement precedes an attack they should inform the doctor, as it can give valuable information about the seat of irritability in the brain that is causing the condition.

'The fit itself may be a short insignificant affair in psycho-motor epilepsy, although this is by no means invariable. Sometimes a state of confusion exists after it, lasting for a long time. It occasionally upsets the person's awareness of his own life and his surroundings. This type of epilepsy is also sometimes associated with personality changes between the attacks, causing considerable difficulty in home and social life'.

Present medical opinion seems to be that epilepsy itself is not inherited but that a low resistance or threshold is. Some babies' brains may be damaged before birth and so pre-dispose them to attacks. Other babies' are damaged dur-ing birth. There may be a lack of oxygen which, we know, can cause permanent brain injury. Growing children are apt to have all sorts of accidents, hitting or falling on their heads, or they can contract infections or develop small clots on the brain, all of which may result in a form of epilepsy.

'At the other end of life, a number of diseases can lead to fits. The commonest of these is a disease of the blood vessels with haemorrhage or a thrombosis. Another risk that increases in later life is brain tumour which might cause epilepsy. It has only recently become apparent that after the age of 50, epilepsy develops in increasing frequency, with increasing age, and is by no means the rare condition it was once considered in old age.'

Some people have an attack brought on by physical ex-haustion, which may again be related to lack of oxygen but it is well known that exhaustion can trigger off a fit especially in those who have had fits already.

'The onset of menstruation sometimes coincides with the

first epileptic fit in girls. A lot of research has been going on into the changes in body chemistry at puberty and into the possible relation between this and convulsions. But up to the present no definite explanation of this undoubted fact can be given. The emotional changes and conflicts associated with growing up, and particularly with the beginning of menstruation, may well play a part in this.

'This brings us to the last and perhaps the most controversial precipitating factor. Emotional upset. The relation between epilepsy and psychological disturbance has long been discussed and argued. There have been people whose epilepsy appeared to be of psychological origin and who were cured by psychological means, but the majority of cases have a physical basis. Nevertheless, emotion plays an important part in many cases and there is no doubt that anger, frustration, despair and strain have at times not only been the starting point of attacks but have triggered off successive ones. It is extremely important that the epileptic patient sees this in true perspective and then endeavours to face the problems of his life rather than to seek protection from them. A negative approach will lead only to frustration when the world around impinges on him, as inevitably it must, in an apparently harsh and unfeeling manner. This frustration itself may then actually aggravate the condition. Parents too, must remember this when they face the problems of bringing up the epileptic child.'

These are aspects which must be understood by teachers, neighbours and the most casual acquaintances if the needs of people suffering from epilepsy are to be appreciated.

'For a very long time epilepsy has been associated in the popular mind with mental deficiency, and even today many people think that a diagnosis of epilepsy means mental deterioration and increasing dullness. This is a mistaken belief. The very fact that a large number of people suffer from epilepsy means that some of them will be of low intelligence, just as some will be brilliant. We must remember also that as epilepsy is a symptom of many different diseases and injuries affecting the brain, in some cases the condition causing it will at the same time cause mental deficiency.

'This is seen in some cases of severe early injury to the brain which result in impaired intelligence and major epilepsy. Very occasionally, the original disorder of the brain will cause actual deterioration with the onset of fits in a child previously apparently normal. It is important to realise that even in the minority of patients who are retarded, it is not the epilepsy which is to blame, but the condition causing it.

'If an epileptic child is over protected and never allowed to behave like other children in case he should have a fit and be injured, he cannot develop normally. The frustration resulting from such mistaken care can be so great that the child becomes withdrawn and takes so small an interest in life that he appears retarded. Children with only minor attacks are rarely subnormal but, as mentioned previously, frequent *petit mal* can mean that the child loses the thread of his teacher's conversation and so may have poor school reports, even though he is really quite bright. This is only likely to occur if the condition has not been diagnosed and treated.

'Another old superstition associates epilepsy with criminal acts, sexual perversion and violence. If this were true, we would expect to find a high percentage of epileptic people in our prisons. Although it is possible that a small number of chronic epileptics do commit minor criminal acts in somewhat greater proportion than average, these are the exception. Such examples of petty troubles apart, the proportion of prisoners who are epileptic is about the same as in the general population. We can certainly say with confidence that epilepsy is not associated with any form of serious criminal activity.

'Once again, we must return to our first premise, that epilepsy is not a disease but an abnormality of the brain caused by many conditions. Some of these conditions affect the personality, as demonstrated in the psychomotor type of epilepsy. An injury to the temporal lobe may involve that part of the brain associated with emotions, and so the scar that causes convulsions will, on occasion, also produce changes in personality. These often show as aggressiveness, moodiness and intolerance. There may be outbursts of sudden temper, quite out of proportion to the provocation, and the adolescent or young adult with this form of epilepsy may become extremely difficult to live with. Even in these cases it is easy to get a false impression. Although a much larger number of persons with temporal lobe epilepsy have these personality disorders than do sufferers from other forms, it is still only a minority. Temporal lobe disease accounts for about a quarter of all adults with chronic epilepsies, but less than half of them are 'difficult'. Even with these, it is found that a high proportion of them come from broken homes. In fact the proportion of epileptics from broken homes who have personality disorders is more or less the same as for non-epileptics.

'Many people have written about the so-called 'epileptic personality'. Although the term is commonly used, different authors seem to mean quite different things by it and it would be better to drop the phrase altogether.

'It is true that most children who suffer from *petit mal* are unemotional and quiet but they also commonly have fair hair and blue eyes. It is also true that a number of sufferers from major fits are somewhat slow and deliberate in thought and action, tend to be moody and stubborn and somewhat overbearing. These characteristics are by no means peculiar to epilepsy and, in some cases, are aggravated by the conditions created by the illness, such as lack of social contact, difficulty in obtaining and holding a job and similar troubles.

'We can say about personality, as about intelligence, that in some cases it will be impaired by the damage that causes the epilepsy. We must be careful, however, in any individual case, to make sure that the disorder is not the result of social and emotional difficulties rather than fundamental to the brain damage.

'The serious injuries to the brain that on occasion affect intelligence and personality, may also produce physical abnormalities. Thus deformities of the body may be associated with epilepsy if the mal-development affects the brain in such a way. A baby may, for example have a catastrophe at or before birth resulting in mental defect, epilepsy and spastic paralysis.

'These disturbances, whether they are physical or intellectual are only found in a minority of cases of epilepsy. They are caused by the disease, injury or mal-development that also causes the convulsions. In no case will any of these disorders develop because a child or adult starts having fits.'

Considering the prevalence of the disease, our ignorance is amazing. There is no doubt that epilepsy can cause bizarre and dramatic situations. It is disconcerting to talk to somebody who suddenly 'leaves' the scene to enter his own private world or who throws a major fit. If one knows what is happening, there surely is no reason to be frightened. It will pass and nobody, not even the victim, will be much the worse for it.

Nobody would hold it against you if you were hit on the head by a piece of falling masonry. People who suffer from epilepsy get hit on the head from within. It is highly embarrassing for them because they know it disrupts what is going on. It seems unreasonable, to say the least, for us to make them feel even worse. Of course, a major fit can be a confounded nuisance but it can't be avoided—at least, you can't avoid it if it's there. It can however be made a little easier if we who happen to be on the spot take easy practical steps and don't make a major production out of it.

Incidentally, most people who suffer from epilepsy hate being labelled 'epileptics'. They argue that between bouts they are not epileptic but just ordinary people, which is perfectly true. Some of our best known and most popular show business and sports personalities and outstanding business tycoons have epilepsy. Usually they do not talk about it because they have learned that the general public still suffers from misconceptions.

HOW WE CAN HELP

When a person has a fit, keep calm and provide an atmosphere of acceptance for the person when he recovers.

Don't leave him lying in the middle of the roadway or near a fire (obviously). Don't try to restrict his movement.

With a major fit, turn his head slightly sideways and backwards to free the airway and let the saliva flow out.

Don't try to put anything between his teeth—you might break them. A bitten tongue will heal.

Don't be silly and try dramatic stuff like mouth to mouth resuscitation. Just keep him company while he is out and be there to meet him calmly when he comes back. If he can live with his fits, so can you.

CHAPTER SEVEN

Muscular Dystrophy

Muscular dystrophy is a condition where the muscle fibres of the body gradually degenerate and break down, leading first to weakness and then in some cases to complete crippling. Sometimes this is hereditary and in other cases there is still no known cause. There is no cure.

There are various types of muscular dystrophy, i.e. neuromuscular disease, of which the commonest and most severe is the **Duchenne** type. This affects only boys and is hereditary, the gene being transmitted through the mother. The boys appear normal at birth and during infancy but they may have some difficulty in learning to walk. Between the ages of two and five, walking and running become increasingly clumsy. The muscles in the shoulder blades and arms also deteriorate. Then the spine becomes weaker and, by the time the boys are between 8 and 11 years old, they are usually unable to walk or to sit up without a harness or corset. The entire body often becomes grossly distorted.

The muscles of the face, hands and breathing system are the last to be affected but eventually these too fail. The boys usually die between the ages of 16 and 25.

There ar other forms of neuromuscular disease which affect adults and are generally not quite as severe as Duchenne. In some cases, just the face or eye muscles are involved. In others, the shoulder blades and arm muscles and/or the legs are weakened. Each condition can be identified and has its own name eg: the Becker type, limb-girdle type, or Dystrophia Myotonica. Practically all these conditions develop gradually and are usually progressive.

We will concern ourselves mainly with the muscular dystrophy that attacks children because it is the commonest and it is more than likely that we will meet a family with an

MD boy in the course of our lives. The needs of adult MD sufferers will be covered in general chapters such as the one on wheel-chair users.

What does one say to parents who have one or two or more beloved sons who, though perfectly ordinary toddlers, then slowly disintegrate before their eyes? There can be no adequate words.

One couple sadly reported that the vicar crossed the street when he saw them because he did not know what to say.

It is easy to understand the vicar's embarrassment but he was fundamentally wrong in thinking that he had to say something that might console or comfort the parents. All he had to remember was that here was an ordinary couple with ordinary daily experiences. They also happened to have, in this case, two sons who were at different stages of muscular dystrophy. These boys were boys who happened to have MD. It would be ridiculous to overlook the magnitude of the disability, but the family is more than just the personification of a tragedy.

It is true that the parents have to live with the situation 24 hours a day for many years but there are other topics to discuss. Then, if the parents want to talk about the illness they will come round to the subject in their own way at their own time. Almost all want an outlet. They yearn to get some of their troubles off their chests. Too often they are faced with good people like the vicar, whose faces and whole bodies express their own fear of being involved in something that they find 'unbearable'.

The vicar probably justified his crossing the street by thinking 'I wont embarrass them by talking to them.' It is a lovely way out.

But he might be doing his job more efficiently and with more satisfaction for himself if he took the trouble to find out a little bit about muscular dystrophy. Then he could talk with intelligence and genuine interest about what was happening. He might find out how parents lifted growing boys into their wheel-chairs and how the boys were helped to sit as comfortably as possible in those chairs. He might wonder how the toilet needs of the boys were met and how often they had to be turned at night.

He might also find out how the boys spent their days. What were their interests? What sort of schools did they go to? Did they read and how were their books held up? What were their favourite television programmes and did they watch much? Would it be possible for somebody with no previous experience of MD to spend an evening with the boys so that the parents could go out together for a change?

The vicar might wonder whether there were any special problems about clothing the boys. As bodies become deformed, it must also become increasingly difficult to find the right trousers and coats. Did the parents get any help with special laundry needs? The vicar might find out what organizations there were, voluntary and statutory, that might help the family and reduce some of the stress.

He could discuss all these subjects with the parents but he might think even further. How can any marriage survive, not only the emotional battering but the practical daily strain of looking after the physical needs of boys who could never be left alone for any length of time?

How were other children in the family affected? And how much did the vicar think about the boys themselves? They might have muscular dystrophy but that did not mean that they were stupid. They were well aware of their condition and though they had probably come to terms with it (for the young are practical and accept when there is no alternative), they could see the worry they were causing their parents. That is often harder to bear than the physical condition itself.

The boys worry about their parents. At the same time, disabled or not, they are growing up and they feel the need for independence and self-sufficiency. They do not want to be tied to their mothers all the time. They want to get away. They want some privacy and a chance to be themselves. It is often as if they knew they had a lot to cram into a short time. Yet they need their mothers (or somebody) all the time for almost everything. They are at the same time both grateful and resentful.

And the parents are resentful too. They must be! It is a prolonged agony. Too many years go by. This is not what they planned for their children or for themselves. If the boys and the parents try too hard to hide their resentment and frustration, the situation becomes even more tense. A good row can clear the air. The boys, however, tend to feel guilty if they fight with their parents and vice versa. Talking about it with somebody like the vicar can ease things all round.

Obviously, the poor vicar has been used here as a peg on which to hang a not unusual situation. Obviously too, this family is representative of many, many other families with disabled children. Caring neighbours and friends will recognise the symptoms. Incidentally, it is amazing how many families with MD or other similar diseases find that their 'families' somehow disappear. Aunts, uncles, cousins just drift out of the picture. Even grandparents are known to say, 'We make a point of staying away. Don't want to add to their troubles you know.' Interesting!

There is one truth that is slowly evolving as the theme of this book. Whether it is repeated in print or not, it stands out loud and clear, 'People need people.'

It is possible, perhaps likely, that readers will at some point meet an adult or a little girl suffering from some form of muscular dystrophy and because that form has its own particular name, it will not be recognised as a neuromuscular condition. Here are some of the better known names. (Incidentally, isn't it extraordinary how one can live almost a lifetime never hearing of a place, person or illness and then suddenly the same name or word crops up two or three times in quick succession?).

One word that is unlikely to become part of your daily vocabulary is **Facioscapulohumeral** muscular dystrophy which is placed first just because it is such a splendid word. Actually, it is one of the rarest and also most benign forms of MD. It affects the facial muscles, making it difficult to close the eyes. It gives a pouting appearance to the lips. Soon there is difficulty in raising the arms above the shoulders and in lifting objects. In many cases the legs are not involved for a good many years, but when they are involved there is often bilateral foot-drop so that the patients tend to catch their toes in the edge of carpets. It is an hereditary condition.

Limb-girdle muscular dystrophy usually begins in adolescence or early adult life but can start at any age. At first it can affect either the shoulder girdle muscles, making it difficult to raise the arms above the head and to lift objects, or the pelvic girdles making it hard to climb stairs, rise from the floor or get out of a low chair. Sometimes the weakness remains restricted to the upper or the lower limbs for many years before spreading. Most patients with limb-girdle MD survive to a normal age and are able to work for many years after the onset, but many become severely disabled in middle life.

Polymyositis can affect patients of any age and is not inherited. The muscles become inflamed, are often tender and generally weak. Treatment by certain drugs will usually cure this disease but it is nasty while it lasts.

Myasthenia gravis is a condition in which the muscles are not activated properly and fatigue and weakness result. The muscles moving the eyes and face and those involved in swallowing are often particularly affected, though all muscles of the body may be weak in some cases. It is not inherited and in most patients does not produce progressively increasing weakness. There is generally response to treatment.

Dystrophia myotonica or myotonic dystrophy can be seen in the hands especially and consists of slowness in relaxing the grip. The difficulty is worse in cold weather. In addition, the facial muscles become weak so that the patients have difficulty in closing their eyes and in whistling. The neck muscles are also affected. Eventually in most cases the muscles of forearms and those below the knees also become progressively weaker so that increasingly severe disability occurs in middle life. Many males with the condition also develop frontal baldness and cataract often develops prematurely. The myotonia or muscular stiffness, with difficulty in relaxing the grip, can be relieved by appropriate drugs but, as in other forms of muscular dystrophy, the progressive weakness of the facial and limb muscles cannot as yet be influenced by treatment.

There are other diseases which do not primarily affect the muscle, such as diseases of the thyroid gland. The skeletal muscles may become secondarily weak. There is also a group of conditions in which attacks of muscular weakness are associated with alterations in the chemical composition of blood and muscle. These disorders, called the **familial periodic paralyses**, are dominantly* inherited. They can be greatly helped by treatment with various drugs.

In addition, there are a number of rare diseases of muscles grouped under the title **congenital myopathies**. They usually cause muscular weakness with floppiness of the limbs and trunk in the first few years of childhood. There is delay in standing and walking. At present there is no suitable drug.

Just as there are a number of different muscular dystrophies so there are a number of different diseases damaging the motor neurons in the spinal cord. The most severe form is infantile muscular atrophy (sometimes called **Werdnig-Hoffman disease**) in which the child becomes affected either before birth or within the first six months of life. The child is usually limp and floppy and the weakness generally progresses rapidly. Other similar but less severe diseases can arise in older children and adolescents (sometimes called **Kugelberg-Welander disease**), or in adults. Here the progress of the disability is slower. Patients may be able to work for many years after the onset, though many become severely disabled in middle-life. Sometimes the disease seems to become arrested.

Scapuloperonal muscular atrophy is one of the forms of the later onset spinal muscular atrophies. No drugs have any influence upon the progress of the disease but physiotherapy and attention to posture in order to prevent limb deformity and contractures play an important part in management. Appliances may be helpful in individual cases.

*See chapter 14

All these names and technical details are unnecessary mental clobber for most people. Each of those names and far, far more details are of infinite concern for the particular patients and their families. Everybody is better equipped to be useful and understanding if he or she has some idea of what a general term like muscular dystrophy is all about.

Even trained highly qualified nurses have been known to leave a child or perhaps an adolescent on a toilet with instructions to sit straight—as if they could! This is just one example of typical thoughtlessness which could be avoided.

Maybe the slogan, 'People need people.' is not enough. Perhaps it should be 'People need people who understand their needs.'

CHAPTER EIGHT

Old Age

Younger people tend to think of the old as a special breed. They're not. The old are simply young people who have lived a long time and find themselves with bodies that are wearing out. To themselves they are still the same people that they always were.

Few men and women actually enjoy getting old. It is no fun to have sight and hearing fail and to find that your skin does not fit as well as it used to. Blood circulation is not what it was and you feel the cold more. Energy wanes, stairs become steeper and loads heavier. Rheumatism and arthritis cause pain and stiffness. There is not much you can do except learn to live with it. The alternative, as some wit remarked, is even less attractive.

All this would be bad enough but you also have to contend with the general public and too often one can include family in the general public. They tend to be impatient, critical, patronising, intolerant and utterly intolerable. They treat an old person as if the symptoms of age were his or her fault, as if there had been a deliberate choice to become slower, less competent and more absent-minded.

Some younger people, especially the middle-aged, approach the old with obvious condescension and overbearing sweetness. 'Look! He can still talk. Isn't he clever? Bless him.' It is as if every man and woman over a certain age automatically became a blithering idiot.

Some old people do become blithering idiots. Some are blithering idiots all their lives and they are not going to change in their old age. In fact, observation shows that not only are old people the young people they were, but they tend to be more so. Characteristics, traits, foibles become stronger and more exaggerated, perhaps because there are fewer influences to suppress or control them. Less is expected of the old and so they relax.

One might say that the old, having lived a lifetime, are entitled to their relaxation. If you take the attitude that the old have done their whack and nothing more should be expected of them, then you are also saying that the old are not needed. You imply that they have nothing to offer, that the world can do very well without them. They become rejected.

The old, like all other human beings, do not like to be rejected. It hurts and is resented. They are still the same people they used to be. They used to have responsibility and importance. Now they have none. Many retain their old skills and abilities but these are now unwanted. It is extremely annoying and so the old, quite justifiably, get the reputation of being bad tempered, irritable, resentful and, worst of all, boring. They do go on so.

If nobody expects anything from you, if you are rejected, you just might have the guts and energy to fight back and you might win. There are lots of people who have lived a very long time but who are still thoroughly involved in their work and in their relaxation. They live 70, 80 or a 100 years but whatever changes the years may have brought, they remain in charge, they master the handicap.

There are others, however, who may never have learned to fight or whose physical condition may make fighting impossible. Physical changes that occurred with increasing age may have changed their personalities and their capacity to think. This does happen. And when you get the old relaxing because they have not got the energy to fight the attitudes that surround them, then you get the type of 'relaxation' that shows they just do not care any more.

They do not wash as frequently as they used to and their clothes are not changed as often. They may be slightly incontinent but can't be bothered to do much about it. If they feel flatulent, they will belch or pass wind. If there is a drop at the end of their nose, they leave it there. There may be hair growing out a wart on the chin but they do not bother to look in the mirror and don't even try to pull it out. Food becomes their major interest. They may eat noisily and with total concentration. They become caricatures of the men and women they once were.

This reaction to rejection may well be exacerbated by insufficient money. You cannot be clean and tidy if you cannot afford laundries or soap powders. You lack energy if you are cold because you cannot pay for power or fuel. It is a vicious circle.

Many of them are scared, scared of dying. Their friends and contemporaries disappear. They are lonely and uninvolved and have too much time to think about themselves—how much they have lost, how little they have and a future that looks bleak. Some find comfort in religion and, at least, have the involvement of their beliefs. Others do not have even that.

The answer is obvious and some cultures provide it. But western civilisation, for all its technical brilliance and economic complexities, has on the whole fallen down on its treatment of the old. It is not just an economic problem to be solved by doling out higher old age pensions, though that is preferable to letting the old starve or freeze to death. Until we have found a way of accepting the aged as an integral part of our society, until we have found a way of making them as useful as they are capable of being, we ought to be ashamed of ourselves. Even if they can only sit and tell stories of the past to the young, then the value of those stories should be appreciated and shown to be appreciated.

Old age can be a terrifying disability. But 95 per cent of the time, it is our standards and our way of living that has made it so.

What, then, can the individual do? Many old people are fairly satisfied if they get just a little company, a little contact with other human beings. Many are so used to being alone that they find being with others delightful for a short time, but not for too long. Talking becomes a strain. Others can't get enough company and no matter how much they get want more. It is obvious that their greatest satisfaction comes from talking about their resentment and grievances. Fair enough; if that is what makes them happy, so be it. One listens to their grumbles, tries to ensure that they are warm, comfortable and have enough to eat and leaves it at that.

But many old people want an opportunity to contribute whatever they can. These are the men and women who respond and blossom when they are allowed to 'do their thing'. This is where the caring individual can fulfil a need—not by doing anything for the old but by supplying opportunities for the old to do things. Let them participate! They are often excellent at helping other old folk who are not so capable. They are often first rate with children. Time and time again, a sympathetic old person can make contact with even the most rebellious teenager whom nobody else can handle. There are innumerable essential jobs that are a waste of time for highly qualified workers in any number of fields which the old could take on as voluntary or part-time employment. It would be a help for all. It may sound harsh but often the best thing you can do for the old is to make use of them.

Years ago, in our society, and even now in some parts of the world, old age was accorded reverence and respect. The old could throw their weight about with no one to say them nay. Nobody ever seemed to question why in the world one should respect a person just because he had not died. Old people can be stupid, self-centred, greedy, dishonourable. Should one really respect them because they happen to be 80 years old? But the pendulum can swing too far the other way. Just because a person is 80 is no reason for treating him or her as unacceptable. Living a long time is not a crime.

There should be no need to enumerate the practical assistance which is invaluable to the old and infirm. Shopping, transport, laundering, gardening, housekeeping, decorating, often require more energy and agility than old bodies can supply. Help is appreciated. Sometimes it is given cold bloodedly and distantly as if the person for whom the work was being done just did not exist. That devalues the help.

The old, too, are people who need people who understand their needs.

It seems important to make one more point. There are ageless men and women who actually, with passing years, become increasingly attractive. They usually share certain qualities. They are good-natured, they show a greater interest in others than in themselves and they are adaptable in action and thought.

This is not a lesson that can be forced on any bad tempered, self-centred, rigid old crone but while this book is being written and later read, time is passing and everybody is getting older.

The point had to be made.

CHAPTER NINE

Incontinence

It is no sudden revelation that we cannot choose what is wrong with us. Things just happen. Nobody asks for failing sight or hearing, a dicky heart, arthritis, multiple sclerosis or any of the other conditions that make life so much more difficult. Least of all does anybody want to be incontinent, to lose control of bladder and/or bowel.

The need for this control is fundamental for acceptance in any society from the Poles to the Equator, from the most primitive tribes to the most sophisticated urban societies. Universally, we accept that babies soil themselves but, as soon as they are toddlers, they are disciplined to control where and when they urinate and defecate. Nowhere, not even in the remotest jungle, is it tolerated that people foul their homes. This is basic to mankind.

So what are we expected to do about the large number of older children, men and women, who suffer from conditions causing incontinence? The conditions are many and varied. They may be due to spinal lesions, muscular weakness, surgical intervention, emotional or neurological disorders, senility. The incontinence may be minor, a slight dribble of urine, to total with constant or spontaneous bowel evacuation.

This may be the only presenting symptom. Otherwise the sufferer may be mobile, energetic, efficient, intelligent, charming. It may be part of more far-reaching damage as in Spina Bifida. It may be just an added insult to the unwelcome deterioration that comes with old age.

An 'accident' causes utter embarrassment for all concerned. It is breaking the most fundamental rule of social acceptability.

Many victims of Multiple Sclerosis become incontinent

and one of the greatest boons of meetings of their Society is that members can joke among themselves about their inevitable lapes. They all understand.

There are deeper implications than just embarrassment. The victims feel 'dirty'. They often smell strongly and others want to keep away from them. They want to get away from themselves. Medical treatment may improve or cure or circumvent the condition. Our concern is with the situation as it exists and what can be done practically to make it a little easier for those who are lumbered with it. Probably this can best be done by tackling the 'dirty' element.

A lack of bladder control is obviously easier to tackle in men than in women. Appropriate sacks or bags can be worn in relative comfort and can be emptied, washed or replaced quite easily. Most women become accustomed at some point in their lives to using sanitary pads. The most important thing is to see that these are changed frequently.

Lack of bowel control presents many more problems. There are all sorts of special garments and gadgets on the market. Health Visitors, doctors, nurses, social workers can give practical advice and some cities provide an incontinence advisory service. Pamphlets and leaflets give information about devices for various conditions and generally include notes on odour control. The trouble too often, is that the victims are too self-conscious to confide in anybody. They try to cope on their own with more or less success. It is sometimes possible for 'outsiders' to lead the conversation, impersonally, on to the facilities that are locally available. What happens after that will depend on the response. Don't force it.

Incontinence is demoralising. It corrodes human dignity. People often tend to give up. They stop trying. If you are old and lacking in energy anyway, you just cannot be bothered. Keeping oneself clean uses up effort and money. It is all too much.

Can the community, can families or friends really be expected to overcome the basic instinct to shun the incontinent?

Is it asking too much for ordinary people to ignore what may be an all-pervading 'weakness' and to concentrate on, appreciate and respect the rest of the personality? Probably!

We might however be able to exert just a little more self-control (aided and abetted by the excellent space deodorants that are now generally available). If our guest should have an accident and leave a stain on a carpet or chair, it can always be cleaned. It is much more difficult to mend a person's self-esteem.

Here is just another condition over which the patient has no control. He surely should not be blamed or shunned for it. It can happen to anybody.

CHAPTER TEN

The Deaf

Many people think that if you are deaf, you cannot hear. This is not strictly true. The vast majority of 'deaf' people can hear some sounds. They are, on the whole, called deaf when they cannot hear as well as other people do.

Sometimes an after-dinner speaker will not talk loudly enough and the audience will shout, 'Speak up.' They know that although they are not deaf they cannot be expected to hear indistinct sounds. There may be one or two with exceptionally acute hearing who have caught every word. Those sitting nearest the speaker may have been all right but the further sound travels, the more it is reduced so that those sitting at the back of the room heard little or nothing. There may be somebody sitting almost on top of the speaker who could not hear what was said because his hearing was not as good as his neighbours. He is deaf.

He may wear a hearing aid which amplifies sound and with the aid, he may hear as well as anybody else. On the other hand, his hearing loss may be so severe that, even with the strongest hearing aid, he hears only a muffled rumble or nothing. He may therefore have learned to rely on his eyes rather than his ears and be dependent on lip-reading the speaker in order to understand what is being said. This is not easy but it can be done. Many people with a moderate hearing loss combine what they are able to hear with what they are able to see, the one sense supporting and co-operating with the other, and they get along very well.

If the hearing loss is severe, then the hearing aid will have to be very strong and amplify sound to a great degree. If you amplify a sound too much you also distort it. We all know that if a radio or television set is turned up too high, the result is not loud music or speech but just plain noise. Some deaf people who use strong hearing aids, have taught themselves to recognise the distorted sounds which they can get. In some ways, it is like learning a new language.

It is common for men and women to lose their hearing as they get older. Sometimes deterioration sets in at a very young age. It can be a big problem. It is a great hardship for they still want to participate in what is going on. They want to chat with friends and they can't. Being deaf they do not hear what is said and they look blank and appear stupid. They are treated as if they were stupid. They become frustrated and bad tempered. They are told to wear a hearing aid. They try.

The amplified sound they get with an aid does not sound a bit like speech as they remember it. They are often too old to learn this new language which they are hearing. The aid is put in a drawer. Useless.

Somehow they have to come to terms with a world that is going about its business leaving them out. Deaf people are rejected and isolated. They turn to books and watch television. They often turn the sound up so high that it disturbs everybody else. They are very lonely.

Some try to convince themselves that they are not really deaf and they shout and bully their families and friends. Quite a few seem to think that if they do all the talking, then nobody else will be able to speak and their deafness will go unnoticed. It works to a certain extent but they do become the most awful bores. Incidentally, it's extraordinary how many deaf people, even children, hate to admit how deaf they are. They often bluff giving the impression that they have understood a situation or a question, but actually haven't got a clue. Don't try to catch them out but do make certain that they really know what it is all about and are not just nodding agreement in total ignorance.

Deafness is an infuriating disability. Apart from being socially unacceptable, it has enormous practical disadvantages. It usually interferes radically with any work the person may be doing and is therefore economically threatening. Daily life becomes much more difficult, especially if the person is too deaf to use a telephone. Shopping, even in self-service stores, becomes an ordeal. Sometimes the total figures on the cash register at the pay-out desk are large and clear but sometimes they are hard to see and the girl at the check-out point mumbles. There is no time for patience.

Travelling by air, rail or sea involves endless announcements of alterations and directions which become a threatening nightmare for the deaf who are never able to relax. If you cannot hear properly, you do not know when you have dropped your keys or when the kettle is boiling. When driving (and the deaf are often exceptionally good drivers because they have learned to be constantly alert), they cannot switch on the radio for traffic news. There are a thousand and one little irritations that add up to a massive handicap.

With advancing age, the loss of hearing is usually gradual but occasionally, due to illness or surgery, there is a sudden dramatic and total loss of hearing. Those who are profoundly deaf cannot hear their own voices. That is why they often shout. (Any woman who has ever been under a noisy drier at the hairdresser will know the embarrassment when the drier is switched off and she realises that she has been shouting at the top of her voice because she could, literally, not hear herself speak.)

If you lose the ability to monitor your own voice, it becomes distorted and many deaf people have a flat and peculiar way of speaking. They are often unaware of this because they cannot hear themselves.

Mrs J had become increasingly deaf since the age of 20. She was an attractive, vivacious, busy woman. With her particular condition there was a chance that an operation might restore her hearing. There was a slight chance of failure and she knew it. Nevertheless she thought it was well worth the gamble. In the event, things went wrong and Mrs J ended up with practically no hearing at all. She had to readjust her entire life. She knew her voice was affected. Despite speech therapy, she sounded 'different'. Bitterly she complained—'I know I'm still me but, because my hearing has gone, I've become a freak. I'm not a freak; I'm myself, but I seem to be the only one who knows it.'

Some severely deaf adults join clubs for the hard of hearing or deaf and some take the time and trouble to learn signing and/or finger spelling. These are manual means of communication. In signing, a hand movement or position symbolises a word or concept. We all know that thumbs up means good. For some reason the 'deaf' sign for bad is not thumbs down but the little finger up. The thumb crossing the forehead means 'to think'. With finger spelling, each word is spelled out using either the two-handed or one-handed alphabet. In the USA the latter is prevalent but in Great Britain, both hands are still generally used. (See illustrations on pages 56/57).

The trouble is that a relatively small community can communicate in this way and it is therefore socially restrictive. Also most older people usually do not want to bother to learn a new technique. Another factor comes into it, too. Men and women who lose their hearing become constantly and increasingly frustrated and this makes many of them irritable and short tempered. Put a lot of tetchy people in the same club and they are unlikely to create a warm and loving atmosphere. Each one desperately needs sympathy and patient understanding. They are not the ones to give it to each other.

The child who is born deaf or who loses hearing early in life, is faced with completely different problems. We all learn to talk by imitating what we hear. If nobody ever speaks to a child with normal hearing, the child will not learn to speak. If the child is surrounded by people who speak German, he will learn to speak German and if they are all talking Chinese, he will learn Chinese. The children who cannot hear speech will not learn to talk. A child is never born 'deaf and dumb'; he becomes dumb because he is deaf. It is as simple as that.

The word 'dumb' is so identified with the word stupid that it is, understandably, highly unpopular. It hurts parents to

have their children referred to as deaf and dumb. Later it
hurts the deaf themselves. Apart from the undermining
implications, most deaf children and the adults they
become, try to talk and don't consider themselves 'dumb' in
any meaning of the word.

Very few children have no hearing at all. Almost all have
some residual reaction to sound. That is why they are
supplied with hearing aids at the earliest possible age. It is
exciting to see a baby in a pram, wearing his aids, hearing
sounds for the first time, his eyes opening wide at the wonder
of it all. Here is a new experience. He will not recognise or
understand what he hears. That will come with time and
practice. At first the very sensation of hearing is thrilling.

Almost all children who are born deaf have what is known
as nerve deafness. With the present state of medical
knowledge, there is still no cure for this condition. This is an
accepted fact but a most difficult one for parents to swallow.
They usually keep looking and hoping. Some day
undoubtedly an answer will be found. Till then all our efforts
must be directed towards ensuring that deaf children have
some means of communicating. They must be able to
understand what is said to them, they must be helped to
express themselves. Otherwise they will, from infancy, be
handicapped intellectually, emotionally, socially and
eventually economically. Again this is an accepted fact.

There is still, however, controversy as to the best way to
give a deaf child language. With the improvements in
hearing aids and other technological developments, there
are many who believe that it is possible to teach almost all
hearing impaired children to make maximum use of
whatever hearing they do have; that they can be taught to
speak and to lip-read and to regulate their voices. There are
others who think it is preferable to teach them to sign and
finger-spell and learn, where feasible, to talk at the same
time. These arguments are for the parents and the experts.
They need not plague or concern the next door neighbour or
friend.

It does not really matter whether a deaf boy or girl has

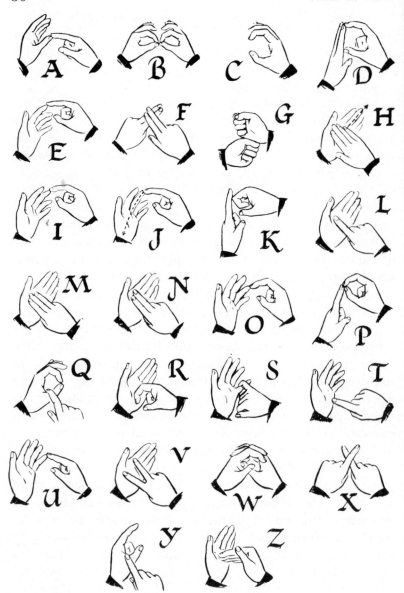

This is the two-handed manual alphabet used for finger spelling to the sighted deaf in Great Britain and many parts of the world. Note how each symbol forms, or at least suggests, the letter it represents.

THE ONE-HANDED MANUAL ALPHABET

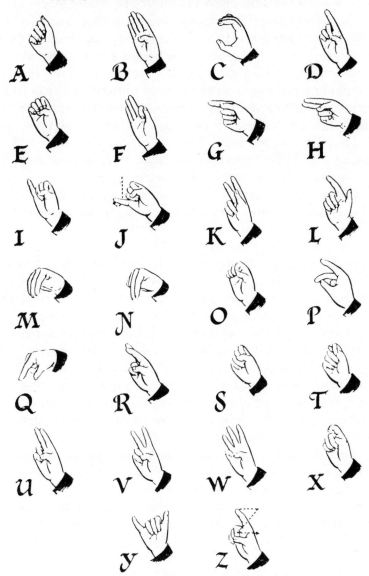

This is the one-handed manual alaphabet used for finger spelling to the sighted deaf in some other parts of the world including the United States of America. Although there are occasional resemblances, the symbols are not so clearly related to the written letter shapes, nor can they so easily be read at a distance.

learned to talk, is learning to talk or can't talk. All we are
concerned with is that here is a child who would like to play,
let you know about his troubles, show you what interests him
or find out what interests you. Everybody likes friends. Deaf
children do too, but cruelly few people can be bothered to
make friends with a deaf child. It is not always easy. It takes
time to find out how you can best communicate. They often
make ugly incomprehensible noises when they are trying to
talk. They are deaf and do not know that they sound peculiar
and nobody can tell them. They desperately want to tell you
something. It is important to them. People turn away in
embarrassment, sometimes in disgust.

There is no doubt that some disabilities are less
unattractive or more socially acceptable than others. Deaf
children look perfectly normal and that is why it is often a
shock when they sound so odd and behave strangely.
Nobody has been able to explain to them the things that are
'done' and the things that are not 'done' because they could
not hear the explanations. And they could not read the
answers in a book or paper because you cannot read unless
you know the words you are reading. Can you read Turkish?

When one reflects how unbelievably difficult growing up
must be for a child who has never heard the human voice, it
is almost miraculous that the vast majority manage to
become adults who are responsible citizens, capable of
holding responsible jobs and becoming responsible parents
of respected families. The odds are stacked against them
because so many people cannot be bothered to get involved.

Can we help deaf adults? They fall into two categories—
the deafened—those who lost their hearing later in life when
they were able to talk, read, write and understand language,
and those who are born deaf or are pre-lingually deaf.

In the past, it was easy to tell them apart. Those who lost
their hearing still retained their grammar, flow and
understanding of language. Their behaviour too was more
ordinary. Why not? They were ordinary people who had
gone deaf.

The pre-lingually deaf rarely spoke at all and were more

likely to make unintelligible noises. Many had small vocabularies and a restricted knowledge of language so that even their written communications were of subnormal standard. There were exceptions, of course, whose written language was perfect and whose speech could be understood if one made an effort and became accustomed to it.

Nowadays the situation has become more confusing. Many who were born with a severe hearing loss, have been taught to speak fluently and almost normally. Many sound slightly 'foreign'. They make maximum use of hearing aids and lip-reading. They are found in professions such as law, architecture, accountancy, surveying. They still can't hear but they are much more like those who were deafened rather than born deaf.

Unfortunately these are still exceptions. The majority of those born deaf still speak badly even though they may have achieved high academic or professional standards. If you meet a deaf person, you still have to 'play it by ear'. The easiest approach may be to smile and ask outright, 'How deaf are you? What do you want me to do to make it easiest for you?'

He or she will be delighted to tell you and, if that was not possible, you will have learned that miming and writing may be your best way to exchange ideas. Do try to remember to smile, or, better still, make sure that you feel like smiling. The deaf are faced with too many scowls.

The deaf need one to one attention. Don't try to get them into a group discussion. It generally will not work. If, however, you know that a person in a group is deaf, make a point of personally letting him know what is going on. Tell him when the topic of conversation changes, give him the main points. He may be able to pick up 50 per cent of the gist himself. With your help, he will get it all or most if it.

If the deaf person says something that is out of context and right off the track, try not to make him feel an ass or a nuisance. Just put him in the picture. And try not to be patronising either. Ask for his opinion and listen to what he has to say. It may not be any more intelligent or constructive than what anybody else has to say. On the other hand, it might be. He deserves a chance to have his say.

Lip-reading has been mentioned quite often. It is not a precise term. The deaf do not read only your lips. They take in your entire face and body looking for clues so they can understand you. Make it easier for them. Be expressive not dead-pan. Smile, scowl, sneer, sniff, laugh—let your face show the mood of what you are saying and use your hands to gesture hints on what you are discussing. Enjoy it. Let it be fun.

One hears some silly twits saying, 'I haven't a very expressive face,' or 'My voice is naturally low.' The only answer is 'Well, start having a bit of expression. Start raising your voice. The face and the voice belong to you. You're in charge. Make the effort.'

If people feel that all the effort should be made by the deaf (or other disabled) then they should just stay out of the way. They only make life more complicated.

As mentioned before, many of the born deaf use manual methods of communication and it is asking too much for the ordinary man in the street to learn any of these methods. But if you do feel like taking it up it is usually most rewarding. It is easy to learn to 'send' messages in no time at all. To be able to read at the speed some manual communicators use is another matter. They will slow down to suit you. (Suddenly the tables are turned; you are the one with the disability because you cannot communicate as quickly as they can.)

Back to ordinary speech. When you are with a deaf or hard of hearing person, don't talk with your hand screening your mouth or with a cigarette dangling away. If you are a man who sports a beard or moustache, consider whether this makes lip-reading difficult. Ask the deaf person. It's good for a laugh anyway. Do not talk to the back of a deaf person's head. Low lights and candle lit dinners may be romantic but they play havoc with lip-reading. In the dark, the deaf are lost.

In some ways, dealing with a deaf child is easy because they are usually eager to make friends. If he is a small child, get down to his level so he can see your face and then play as you would with any other child. If you are somebody who enjoys children at all, then it is no trouble to enjoy a hearing impaired child or, indeed, most disabled or handicapped boys and girls.

You may come across a distraught mite crying his eyes out because he is lost. Being deaf he will not be able to tell you his name or where he lives. Look to see whether he is wearing an identity disc round his neck or wrist and, before taking any practical steps, try to comfort him. When you have gained his confidence, look together for the parent or guardian. Frenzied mothers usually turn up pretty quickly. They have had these crises before. Because of the handicap, they cannot yell for their children as other mothers can.

Parents of deaf children, especially the mothers, live in constant stress. The boys and girls are demanding, stubborn and irresponsible because they do not know the consequences of their actions and can't be told.

Most parents suffer for years from the shock of learning that their ordinary looking child has a major defect. The child's inevitable unusual behaviour and the agony of wondering what the future will hold for him are other problems.

Deaf children rarely need your help but their parents always do. It may be a shoulder to cry on or ears to listen, or baby-sitting for an hour, or just a word of encouragement.

The young deaf child does not know that there is anything wrong with him. He is just himself. It is not until he is well over six years old that the average deaf child realises that he is not like others. By then, with good guidance and a little luck, he should have enough language to understand that his deafness is just one of those things, a confounded nuisance but one which should not interfere with his having a jolly good life. He will prove this to be true, but the parents are still hurt and worried. You can do a lot to put their minds at ease—at least a little.

The best way anybody can help the deaf is to remember that the chief problem is not lack of hearing but difficulty in communicating. If you take the time and trouble to work out together the best way of exchanging ideas, it will be greatly appreciated. Many deaf boys and girls, men and women, seem unattractive at first. They are all lonely whether they admit it or not. When you get to know them better, you may find that you have gained a perfectly ordinary and rather nice friend.

CHAPTER ELEVEN

Phenylketonuria or PKU

You may meet a mother who tells you that her child is suffering from PKU. In the event, she will probably use the full word Phenylketonuria which will have become part of her daily vocabulary since it was diagnosed. Not all that many years ago this would have implied a tragedy, for babies born with this inherited condition looked normal but were unable to cope chemically with ordinary food, became brain damaged and died.

This is a happy story. By special blood test, the condition can now be confirmed before the infant is a month old. The diet can be adjusted to meet the child's needs and all is well. There is a substance called phenylalamine which is part of many foods and is essential to our bodies as salt or water. Normally, this substance is assimilated and turns into proteins and other useful substances but in the PKU child this does not happen. He cannot convert the phenylalamine and when there is too much of the stuff, for too long, it affects the brain and causes damage and mental retardation. The answer is to provide a diet that contains as little phenylalamine as possible. That is not difficult.

In practice, it can be a nuisance and a bore. It is hard on a youngster not to eat the goodies which his playmates are scoffing. it takes a lot of self-discipline which normally can only develop with time. The silly thing is that as the child gets older and does learn the self-discipline, the chances are that he may be able to drop the special diet. Regular checking is necessary. If friends, relatives and neighbours understand what PKU means, they will not be tempted to buy ice creams or chocolate bars as special treats. They will find out what the diet allows—and this may well vary from child to child—and co-operate.

CHAPTER TWELVE

Multiple Sclerosis

There is a knock at the door. You say 'Just a minute.' You get up, go to the door, turn the handle and open it. This is not a complicated operation but it is full of decisions you make and orders you transmit to various parts of your body. Each of your orders is automatically obeyed and each operation is carried out through your central nervous system and its complicated network of nerves. Each of these nerve fibres has a sensitive protective covering, a myelin sheath.

If anything happens to the sheath, the nerve fibres are unprotected and vulnerable. They become damaged and unable to fulfil their normal functions. Instead of obeying our directions, they cause discomfort, sometimes severe pain and leave us no longer in control.

This is what happens in multiple sclerosis. The myelin sheath is damaged or destroyed and the nerve fibres are then unable to do what is normally expected of them. Limbs become weak and eventually useless; balance is lost; speech may become slurred; sight may be affected. It may be impossible to distinguish heat from cold. There may be cramp, pain, pins and needles—all because the nerve fibres are no longer adequately protected by the myelin covering.

Sometimes the sheath repairs itself and any particular problem vanishes or is improved. So far, nobody knows what causes the destruction or the repair. Certain diets and treatments seem to help some cases but there is still no confirmed cause or cure.

Multiple sclerosis (sclerosis mean hardening or turning to bone from the root sklera = bone, as in skeleton) can be vicious, ruthless, slow and horrible. It can also be slow, self-repairing and almost benign. Often there is a period of deterioration followed by remission. Each case is different and all sufferers have hope. That is the one great redeeming feature.

When the diagnosis has been confirmed, the patient is inevitably frightened and shocked. It is a body blow for the entire family. There will always be deep depression but there will also be some hope.

Friends and neighbours who come in like jolly rays of sunshine will be inviting violence. At the same time, sackcloth and ashes will be out of place. What is needed is plain common sense expressed in terms of practical help. Lending a shoulder for tears may be practical and so might a really good cursing session. MS is nothing to be nice about; some strong invective is justified and might as well be enjoyed.

The patient should always be allowed and encouraged to do as much as he can for as long as he can but, as the disease progresses, he will become more and more incapacitated. Constant care will be the order of the day but that care need not require trained nursing. Both the patient and the person looking after him are likely to see too much of each other and both may need a break. In some cases the patient may be on his own too much. New conversations, new interests may be a breath of fresh air. Any friend can take over from time to time. Practical tasks like shopping will have to be done. There may be no home help and this can mean choosing between neglecting the patient or the house-keeping. Any friend can solve that one. Everybody needs companionship. Good talk and a bit of gossip may be welcome.

As with most crippling diseases, financial resources are often affected. Everybody likes little luxuries or outings. Again, as with other progressive conditions, people often get into certain habits of living and are too close to see small changes and improvements that could make life easier. A new pair of eyes can often spot just where a hand rail might be a good idea or how raising a chair could make a difference. This does not give a visitor *carte blanche* to turn the place upside down and inside out.

Jack M enjoyed smoking but could no longer hold a

cigarette. It was actually his mother-in-law, an ardent anti-smoker, who fixed the lighted cigarette between the prongs of a wide fork which was solidly fixed in a glass she had filled with melted wax from old candles. It was set in a tray in front of him. It was not the most brilliant of inventions but it served its purpose well.

It was she who remembered the baby alarm system which had been put aside as her grandchildren grew up. With new batteries it still worked splendidly giving Jack's wife new freedom in her kitchen without leaving him abandoned.

A disability is never fun but outwitting its nasty effects can be very satisfying.

As with most disabilities, the best advice on what to do or not do comes from the afflicted themselves. A beautiful, young MS lady called Jean wrote an article which has already been published in two professional journals and we have permission to quote from it.

'MS can affect most parts of the body but it need not affect the sense of humour. And there are times when human weaknesses and strengths appear more clearly to sufferers. Like a 'good dog' we are often forced to 'sit' and this can have its blessings. It is a good position from which to observe fellow beings. And wheel-chairs can work wonders at exhibitions and crowded gatherings where any disagree-ability can be countered by the threat of run-over feet.

'Don't think I in any way scorn or belittle the help we get. It's all appreciated, but I can't ignore the different ways people offer assistance. There are the *elbow flexers* who, perhaps from timidity or previous rebuffs, can't make up their minds whether to offer me an arm to lean on or not. They diffidently flex their elbows a few times and give the impression of a one-winged duck trying to take off. Then there are the *walkers on top of you* who walk so close you have to concentrate on skirting them to avoid tipping yourself bustle over hairpins. Others the *heavies*, shove their arms through yours and almost pull you down. But my pet horrors are the *hearty brigade* who chivvy you along with cries of 'cheer up', 'come along now', 'you're doing fine' and such little noises.

Best by far are the people who detect the hazard, take action and go their way without asking for thanks or affirmation that they've done 'the right thing'.

Struggling along the pavement one day, with my stick flying in all directions, I remembered how our faces reflect our inner feelings. And my face offered no cheer to the on-coming public. I decided, despite the heavy going I was making, I would smile brightly, look carefree and whistle— like Anna in *The King and I*. My grin and whistle both disappeared when two passers-by tut-tutted about my being sloshed at 9.15 in the morning. So much for cheering the nameless crowd.

Funny ironic is the way we bring a little light into the lives of traffic wardens. Theirs is an unpopular pursuit and we give them a chance to be kind-hearted and generous. They usually grab the opportunity.

We don't seem to so the same for shop assistants. Those in the superior stores often try to avoid confrontation with us by hiding behind pillars or pretending to be customers critically handling goods on display. A bustling street market can be more welcoming. Once when I arrived at a fish stall before the proprietor had finished laying out his wares, he told me to come back in 15 minutes. When I did I was greeted by a long queue. I patiently waited my turn only to be heartily ticked off once more and told never to queue again. I was to stand on the other side of his stall, slip him a wink and he would serve me as soon as he could. Now I get wonderfully fresh fish at about a third of the price I would have paid in a store. And a heart-warming giggle thrown in.

'I used to think MS, the shortened form of the name of our disease, was rather twee, like saying WC or toilet instead of lavatory but I suppose that multiple sclerosis is quite a tongue twister. For the patient MS can present a labour of Sisyphus, but sense of humour, or euphoria, can lessen the burden of pushing that huge stone to the top of that steep hill.

'But please, doctor, hurry with the answer.'

Follow that!

Friedreich's Ataxia

Friedreich's ataxia can easily be mistaken for multiple sclerosis for some of the effects are much the same. This is, however, a genetic condition—see Genetics page 77. It is much less common than MS and does not vary as much in its relentless progress. With MS one never can tell what will happen next. Unfortunately this is not true of FA (Incidentally, there is a registered charity called the Friedreich's Ataxia Group and its initials are a constant source of joy to its members.)

The condition usually manifests itself about the time of puberty. There is a lack of balance, awkward gait and increasing clumsiness. There is a gradual slurring of speech. Simple tasks become impossible and new techniques must be learned to cope with daily life. There is no mental deterioration. The disease is not a killer but the entire body becomes debilitated and most patients eventually die because the heart cannot cope.

As with many of these genetic conditions, the parents are usually perfectly healthy and completely unaware of the enemy within. The rotten thing is that if one child develops the symptoms, it is more than likely that the siblings will too. There is then the agony of waiting and watching. In this respect it is like muscular dystrophy. Because of the slurred speech, strangers may get the impression of brain damage or mental retardation. Not at all. It is a purely neuro-muscular deterioration. Naturally some sufferers are more intelligent than others just as some are better looking than others and some have a more acute sense of humour. All of them need guts.

CHAPTER THIRTEEN

The Mentally Handicapped and IQs

We all know people who are much brighter than we are. They think more quickly; they learn more easily; they have better memories. We also know people who are a good deal more stupid than we are. They seem to know nothing; you cannot teach them anything; they forget everything. We generally use the word 'intelligence' to cover these differences.

It seems that we are born with a supply of the stuff and then we use it to greater or lesser effect. Some babies are born with so little that they will never be able to learn to talk, to dress themselves, perhaps even to stand and they will never be 'clean'. They are severely mentally defective and one does not have to be trained to recognise their deficiencies. They used to be referred to as imbeciles, idiots, morons. The terms do not matter.

What matters is that they are somebody's babies. No parent ever wanted a child like that. Still, it is somebody's baby. It exists and it is not rubbish.

How the parents react to such a child is unpredictable but there must be disappointment, anguish and pain. If a stranger trips and falls heavily in the street, it is common practice to go to him, ask about the damage and see if one can help. One lends a hand to help him get up. It is perfectly normal ordinary behaviour to help someone who is hurt.

The parents of a severely retarded child need help too. Of course that applies to parents of all handicapped children but the public is usually particularly callous about the mentally defective or abnormal.

It was at the time of the first world war that psychologists began seriously considering how to measure intelligence. It could not be weighed on scales or laid out in inches or

centimetres. So, starting with children, they observed what
the majority knew and could do at certain ages. If, for
example, the vast majority of babies learn to walk at the age
of 15 months then those who can walk at 12 months are
quicker than the average and those who cannot walk at two
years are well below the average. Walking is just one
particular achievement that might be influenced by many
factors. It must be viewed as part of the total developmental
picture. One must observe dexterity—at what age can he
feed himself with a spoon, with a spoon and pusher, with a
fork, with a knife and fork. Size of vocabulary is a good
indicator of a child's progress. He may be using 20 words
when he is one year old but will use 200 by the time he is two
years old. Even when he is very young, the child can be
tested over a wide field to see how he compares with the
majority of children of the same age.

Let us consider a ten year old boy. His achievement may
be that of an average eight year old. He is slow in his
development. On the other hand, he may be bright and
though he is only ten, he may know and do things common to
the average 12 year old.

It has taken quite a number of words to say this but all this
information can be contained in a simple expression which is
based on an easy formula—achievement age over
chronological age. The boy of ten who functions as an eight
year old is eight over ten which, stated in decimals or
percentage is 80. The boy of ten who can do what a 12 year
old does, is 12 over ten, or 120. A 14 year old who can
perform only as a six year old is six over 14, or 43 plus.

We have turned the simple fractions into decimals
because they are easier to handle that way but this figure is
not a disembodied percentage; it is specifically a ratio or
quotient of his intelligence. Therefore it is an Intelligence
Quotient or IQ. (Anybody with an IQ of 50 is not 50 per cent
intelligent, any more than an IQ of 125 indicates 125 per
cent intelligence. That would not make sense. For many
readers, this is teaching grandmother to suck eggs but there
are an awful lot of people who glibly use the term IQ and

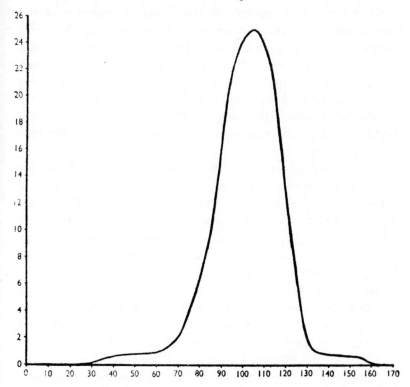

haven't a clue what they are talking about. If you know what the term means, then you will be able to assess its value, dependability and also its fallibility.

When testing adults, the quotient is not achievement age over chronological age but personal achievement over average achievement ie: how does one compare with the norm? Therefore if a child or an adult is said to have an IQ of 100, that means he is average or normal.

A graph of the population spread (above) looks like an inverted ice cream cornet with the few at one end having practically no intelligence at all, the vast mass in the centre around the 100 mark and then tailing off again with a very few being intellectual geniuses. It is obvious therefore that the vast majority are somewhere between 80 and 120 or thereabouts.

It must be remembered that we are not measuring anything as set and objective as weight or length. An ounce is an ounce everywhere and a foot is 12 inches no matter where you go. Here, however, we are dealing with a more abstract and subjective quality, human potential. A stone that weighs 102 kilograms is two kilograms heavier than a stone that weighs 100 kilograms. But a man who is said to have an IQ of 102 is not necessarily two points smarter than one with an IQ of 100.

Many factors must be taken into account. Did he have a cold in his head when he took the test? What sort of education has he had and how much has he been taught to exercise his mind on the types of questions he was asked? How controlled was the test and how experienced the tester? Which of many tests did he take? Is his cultural background comparable to the background of those who set the norm?

In most standard tests, language, numbers and performance are involved. Using language is a great idea because that is the way we usually ask questions and give answers but it is not a good idea to test somebody in English if his understanding of English is limited. Most tests are written and set on paper and this is no use for people who cannot read or write (dyslexics or illiterates) or for those who have communication difficulties like many deaf people, aphasics or foreigners. Non-verbal performance tests can be given.

Though intelligence test results should always be eyed with a certain amount of caution, it is extraordinary how consistent results usually are right through a person's life. A person's intellectual potential seems to remain fairly constant. The important word there is 'potential'. As with every single child that ever was born anywhere in the world, he or she can be helped and guided to make the most of himself or he can be restricted, retarded and wasted.

This is where we hit the age old argument about the relative importance of heredity and environment. Where does the influence of one start and the other end? It doesn't matter. We know that if children go to good schools they learn more than if they go to bad schools or no schools at all. We know that babies abandoned in a forest will grow up crawling on all fours. Unless you are shown what is in good painting, you will not be able to appreciate it. Unless you learn to listen to music, you will not know what it is all about. Unless a lad serves his apprenticeship, he will not have certain skills. A nurse must be taught how to nurse. The mentally handicapped have a restricted potential but that certainly does not mean that they have no potential at all. They must be helped to stretch to their limits.

The mentally handicapped are people and they want to be occupied within the limits of their capacity. They want to do something and be praised when they do it well. They want friends. They want to dance and sing and laugh—unless they are so very handicapped that they do not even know what a want is. Luckily, as our graph shows, these are few, but they too have parents and parents need reassurance and comfort. If the children, no matter what age they are, live at home the parents will need respite, an occasional escape. They want comforting but not patronising. They do not want to be rejected and they do not want their children rejected.

If a boy has an IQ that is not as high as that of most of the other children in his neighbourhood, then all we are saying is that his IQ is not as high as that of other children. It does not make him inferior. Of course he may not be able to contribute quite as much to his community because he has not got the inate ability. If we start evaluating people by the contributions they make then we are on very slippery ground. This is not the place to start comparing the relative value of a doctor, butcher, banker, ballet dancer or rubbish collector.

Here let us spare a quick thought for the child or adult with an exceptionally high IQ. Special abilities and talents can hardly be called disabilities but they certainly can be handicaps. They prevent an easy relationship with the bulk of fellow creatures. They do not make life easier. It is hard to remember sometimes that a genius is a human being too.

We mentioned in passing, the relative value of the people doing different jobs in our community. The price tag that is placed on each and every one depends upon our standards. Where do our priorities lie? Governments, local authorities, official departments have to work within their budgets and the mentally handicapped are usually low on the priority list This means that there is a lot that could be done officially that is not being done officially and because it is not done officially, it often is not done at all. The result is that a large number of mentally handicapped boys and girls, men and women, never have the faintest hope of realising their potential unless their families have taken on that responsibility as well.

This is sometimes done automatically by parents who are just made that way and could not conceive of doing anything else. It is more often taken on by parents who are fully aware of all implications. It is sometimes done reluctantly from a cold sense of duty or even for the sake of keeping up appearances. The duty is sometimes partially accepted or denied altogether.

Whatever the attitude, there is much room for outside help. There is a need for employment, companionship, friendship, game playing, baby sitting, new interests. Almost all these are really within the capacity of anybody who can play with a child. With few exceptions, the mentally handicapped are all children who remain children all their lives.

In Great Britain, the Mental Health Act of 1959 recognises two degrees of mental subnormality 'severe subnormality' and 'subnormality'. Here are the definitions:

Section 4 (2) 'Severe subnormality' means a state of arrested or incomplete development of mind, which includes subnormality of intelligence, and is of such a nature or degree that the patient is incapable of living an independent life or of guarding himself against serious exploitation, or will be so incapable when of an age to do so.

Section 4 (3) 'Subnormality' means a state of arrested or incomplete development of mind (not amounting to 'severe subnormality') which includes subnormality of intelligence, and is of a nature or degree which requires or is susceptible to medical treatment or other special care or training of the patient.

Those who drew up these definitions undoubtedly felt that they were clarifying a situation and facilitating constructive action.

CHAPTER FOURTEEN

A Bit about Genetics: Down's Syndrome, other Chromosomal damage and Restricted Growth

Nobody really knows exactly why there is such a variation in intelligence. The immediate answer, of course, is genes. To start with, we are what we are because our parents were what they were and because they were what their antecedents were. Even the most superficial knowledge of genetics makes a number of conditions easier to understand.

We all know that our bodies are composed of cells. Flesh, bone, muscle, hair, toe nails—every part of the body is composed of masses of minute cells arranged in different patterns and fulfilling different functions. Each of these cells, like a chicken's egg (which is also composed of many cells) has a yolk or nucleus which is surrounded by fluid.

We also know that conception takes place when a specialised male cell (sperm) unites with a specialised female cell (ovum). Each of these cells has a nucleus and this nucleus consists of chromosomes, 23 pairs of them. Each of these pairs consists of genes. It is these infinitesimal genes that determine what sort of a baby will be born. They are responsible for all the hereditary factors in the baby's make-up. It is these genes which determine whether the infant will have brown eyes or blue, whether he will be tall or short, dark or fair, intelligent or dim-witted, liable to certain diseases or not.

As we have said the nucleus of every cell has 23 pairs of chromosomes, so that if a sperm and an ovum unite one would expect to have 46 pairs of chromosomes, but that is too many. What happens is rather miraculous. The sperms grow and multiply in the testes but in their final division, before being ready to fertilize the ovum, they grow to full size but have only 23 chromosomes each. The same phenomenon occurs in the ovum, so that the chromosomes match when fertilisation occurs and, once more, we have 23 pairs which is as it should be.

Some genes are very determined and strong and, when paired off with another gene on the matched chromosomes, they will have their own way. When a gene has this determination or ability to make itself felt, regardless of its partner, it is called a dominant gene.

There are other genes which carry positive characteristics but these genes are not so pushing, and if they are paired off with an opposite gene, they will retire and remain unnoticed. These are called recessive genes. Obviously, it is going to be easier to keep track of the dominant genes because they come to the fore to be noticed whereas the recessive genes are hidden.

When two recessive genes for the same characteristic are paired, there is no conflict or dominance and the characteristic will appear. For example, the gene for brown eyes is dominant, that for blue eyes recessive. When one parent has brown eyes and the other blue, the chances are that the child will have brown eyes. The parent with brown eyes may, however, have had a blue-eyed mother or father or grandparent and will therefore carry a recessive gene for blue eyes. It is possible that this recessive gene will meet the blue-eyed gene of the blue-eyed parent and the child will then have blue eyes.

There are recessive genes for assets and debits, for talents and handicaps. When the recessive gene from the mother and the recessive gene from the father are paired in the offspring, the characteristic, good or bad, will appear. All this explains why marriages of first cousins have been considered dangerous. Since they are closely related, they are more likely to carry the same recessive genes and therefore the odds on an abnormality appearing in their progeny are greater. Genetics is all about the combinations, permutations and mutations that affect genes, dominant and recessive, the result of which is that amazing creature, a baby. There are genetic counsellors who can give expert advice on the probability of any known abnormality appearing in the children of couples who feel they have cause to worry.

This is a brief and totally inadequate description of a colossal field of study.

Now we know that genes basically determine how bright or stupid we are going to be. They determine how dark our skin will be and how big our feet. They also sometimes get together to form an exceptional pattern which becomes recognisable because it occurs, possibly rarely, but frequently enough for familiarity. This formation of a recognisable pattern of symptoms is called a syndrome.

The man in the street can generally recognise somebody suffering from Down's syndrome, more commonly called Mongolism. Here is a pattern or syndrome that includes among many other characteristic features, a large head, short body, short neck, flat nose and slit eyes.

To quote from Dr. Alan Heaton-Ward's book: 'People with Down's syndrome vary widely in their degree of mental incapacity within a wide range of IQ and achievements, including, in some cases, the ability to read and write, but all chromosomally confirmed cases fall within the severely subnormal category judged on the criterion of their inability to lead an independent existence. Their practical ability exceeds their reasoning ability. Most sit by the age of one year and learn to walk between the ages of two and three years. They have an outstanding capacity for mimicry (in which they are no respecters of persons) and it is this which makes them appear brighter intellectually than, in fact, they are. They are affectionate and characteristically cheerful and, although often mischievous, as a group are the most easily managed of all ambulant mentally subnormal patients. They are musical and have a strongly developed sense of rhythm. In spite of their superficial similarity as regards   physical   appearance   and   temperamental characteristics, they show many personal variations and should therefore always be treated as individuals.'

The last clause of that paragraph should be superfluous; it is impossible not to love them if you know them well (and are capable of loving anybody). The difficulty for strangers lies in making the first step to getting to know them.

You may have noticed the words 'chromosomally confirmed' at the beginning of the clinical description. The cause of Down's syndrome lies in an extra chromosome. Exactly why it appears and has this extraordinary effect upon the foetus is unknown but it occurs most frequently with older mothers. As with most generalities there are exceptions. The children are good-natured, co-operative and charming. They are rarely headstrong, stubborn or rebellious. They are, however, not normal and have definite limitations. Also they do not look like other children. The main problems therefore are those of embarrassment (which most parents of handicapped children eventually learn to overcome) and, far more important, worries about the future. Few Down's syndrome boys and girls will grow up to be completely independent, self-sufficient adults. They will always need a protective background. It is usual for children to outlive their parents. There's the rub. Parents who may be in their 60s or 70s living with their Mongol son or daughter who may be 40 or 50, will have a deep affection and care for their offspring—an affection and care unlikely to be duplicated by any other home or institution. This is where the friendship of 'outsiders' can bring a certain amount of peace of mind. As long as the parents know that their child will not be completely rejected or neglected, as long as they know that there is still someone who cares, they will find some inner relaxation.

There are a large number of other genetic or chromosomal variations that cause exceptional patterns often with a bizarre appearance, generally accompanied by varying degrees of mental handicap. Most of these are extremely rare. Each can be medically identified and has its own technical name eg: Mandibulo-oculo-facial dyscephaly

(Hallerman-Streiff syndrome), Cerebro-metacarpo-metatarsal-dystrophy,which is also known as pseudo-pseudo-hypoparathyroidism or Albright's syndrome. Splendid names! It would serve no purpose to go into details in a book such as this. Suffice it to say that these are genetically badly damaged people.

Even though there may be few of them, they are part of our society and their existence cannot be denied. They and their families need acceptance and help. Actually, help is probably the wrong word. It so often implies an almost pious, patronising, superior attitude which is not as hurtful as rejection but is far more sickening. Basically, they are people who are very different due to nobody's fault, certainly not theirs. Being different is not a sin or a crime or an uproarious joke. It should not matter at all. It is the society in which we live that makes 'differentness' so important. It is far easier for people and their families to live with a disability than to face the attitude of those about them. It is these attitudes that are really the handicap.

As an example, there is the case of Charles. He is married, has two most attractive daughters, a position of responsibility and international respect. He is also good company, intelligent and has a voice that can charm the birds off the trees. When he was conceived, something went wrong genetically. Charles' good-looking, rather leonine head is normal size but the rest of him never grew properly. He is just about four feet tall. Mobility is not his problem. His little legs and tiny feet carry him all over the world (helped a bit by planes and trains of course). And all over the world, people stare at him.

Medically, he is a dwarf but he objects to the word. He says it conveys the image of Snow White or circus freaks. He says he is not a freak but just one of the many people of restricted growth.

Most human beings these days are taller than Charles. They are between five and six feet. They have furnished their environment to fit people between five and six feet. Chairs, cars, trains, toilets, stairs, clothes are made to suit average sized people. Charles and others like him do not measure up to those standards.

Because they are smaller than normal, bigger people feel entitled to stare at them, to make crude remarks and often to deprive them of the chance to make their own living in the best way they can. In desperation and resignation, even today, many men and women of restricted growth are compelled to put themselves on display in circuses and side shows. Few rejoice in this refuge. They get little comfort in knowing that one the greatest heart specialists in New York some years ago was a doctor no taller than Charles. They probably get little satisfaction in knowing that Charles and a few others have done well in spite of their size. The few are the fighters and had to struggle to get where they are. Not all people, little or big, are fighters even when aggression might be justified. Anyway a wee person being aggressive might look silly and they want to keep their dignity as human beings. Goodness knows, it's hard to do this if you cannot climb onto a bus without help. That help should be available if they ask for it. It is the attitude of those who can easily give the help which is a greater obstacle than the height of the bus platform.

Should you meet a child or an adult who is obviously the victim of a genetic dirty trick, it is up to you to find out whether your friendliness or help is welcome and how much more of your attention would be appreciated and what form that attention should take.

CHAPTER FIFTEEN

Huntington's Chorea

You will never meet a child with Huntington's chorea. It is a genetic condition that generally makes itself apparent round the age of 40—though about 5 per cent of patients show their first symptoms at 20 and another 5 per cent are not affected until they are about 60 years old. Found equally in males and females, it is an inherited neurological disorder and there are, as yet, no specific tests to confirm its presence or give clues to its possible cure or prevention.

The development of the disease usually follows a fairly set pattern. First there are personality changes. Patients tend to become irritable and unreasonable. Gradually the chorea (uncontrolled movements) sets in. At the start, these may be insignificant and the patient may be able to camouflage them with additional small movements but, as they become stronger, arms and legs may flay about and the entire body may be flung from a chair. Writing, using utensils for eating or shaving, putting on make-up become increasingly difficult if not impossible. At the same time patients become more and more deranged. Domestic life for the entire family is extremely difficult. The prognosis is not good.

Inevitably it is a painfully depressing condition, because patients and families cannot ignore it. They know perfectly well what it is and what its future course is likely to be. It is shattering for a man or woman to be an ordinary member of society with responsibilities, obligations, successes, failures, with pleasures and worries, with children, friends, club memberships and fun and then, slowly, be made aware that he or she is a victim of uncontrollable forces which will lead to the destruction of all that is held dear. The only thing to do is to carry on as long as possible as normally as possible. There is no sense in saying, 'Pull yourself together, dear.' or

'Don't look and it will go away.'

Huntington's chorea is ruthless and the only possible solace lies in gratitude for the years that were good. The later in life that the disease manifests itself, the slower its progress.

Drugs can alleviate the condition. Attention from an understanding, efficient GP can be the greatest support. Otherwise, outside help must come from relatives, friends and neighbours. The shape of that help must depend on the circumstances of each particular case.

CHAPTER SIXTEEN

Mental Illness

The mentally ill are recognised as such when their behaviour deviates from the norm. One uses such expressions as 'He's behaving like a lunatic', 'She is out of her little mind', 'The man is bonkers'. These are statements asserting that the person is not acting normally.

At this point some reader is bound to react with, 'What a rotten definition. What about the sex maniac who behaves perfectly normally but cannot control his strong sexual urges? What about the depressive who behaves in an acceptable way but goes home and commits suicide? Surely they are mentally ill.'

Yes, such people are sick, but they are not recognised as such by friends and neighbours until their behaviour becomes abnormal—until we know that they cannot keep their hands off little girls, or until we find then in a gas filled room. This book is not for psychiatrists, nurses or any professionals working in the field. It is for ordinary people who want to get a better understanding of the disabilities of their fellow creatures. As far as we are concerned, the mentally ill do not conform. They are unpredictable; they exaggerate what is normal. It seems most constructive to consider them in the light of their strange behaviour.

Most of us know people who from time to time become aggressive or amorous, whose speech is slurred, whose gait is unsteady, who might suddenly pick up a brick and hurl it through a plate glass window, who might knock off a policeman's helmet. We have learned to recognise that they have been drinking too much intoxicating liquor and they are drunk. Easy. The effect of the alcohol is to dim their judgement. They behave like lunatics and, we might add to ourselves, they must be lunatics to drink that much.

The smoking of pot (cannabis) has become a social habit in certain communities, though it is generally illegal. Alcohol was illegal the the USA during 'Prohibition' but illegality did not affect its consumption much—just its quality and price. Alcohol is still banned in many places but even in those some people still drink. In the same way, some people smoke cannabis and get high. They get a happy, distorted view of the world which interferes with their clear-sightedness.

There is a small fringe of society which indulges in LSD (lysergic acid diethylamide) a drug that sends them on the most horrific trips where they lose all touch with reality and have been known to kill themselves by jumping out of windows, absolutely convinced that they could fly.

On a very different plane, all divers know that if they go beyond a certain depth, there is a danger of becoming euphoric and behaving irrationally. They may fling off their oxygen bottles and feel like doing a bit of free swimming which, under the circumstances, becomes a fatal indulgence. It is the effect that pressurised oxygen has on them.

It is also known that patients who have tumours on the brain suffer personality changes which make them behave in unexpected ways. They may become quite mad. The same is true of some sufferers from Huntington's chorea. Cirrhosis of the liver will mean that the blood supply to the brain is not as good as it ought to be. Blood carries the oxygen which the brain needs to function properly. There we have an example of the way that a liver condition can cause a mental illness. Aging bodies may produce physical as well as psychological causes of mental illness. Forgetfulness, disorientation, odd behaviour are all symptoms of whatever the cause may be.

And the cause may be purely emotional. Stress, worry, tension, are all words that describe emotional vulnerability. Physically, we are all able to carry some weight, be it shopping baskets or weight lifting equipment. We can carry so much and no more. Most ordinary people can run but there is a personal limit to the distance and the speed. We reach our limits and then collapse. In the same way, all of us can stand a certain amount of stress but when it becomes too much, we collapse. The way we do this differs from person to person.

Some have a good cry, dry their eyes and feel better. Others have hysterics and then feel even worse. Some escape to bed and, after a period of rest and recuperation, are fit enough to take on the strain of living again. Others become totally depressed and lose all urge to live. A few become obsessed with factors that might normally be accepted as unimportant. Stress and the reaction to it affects people's behaviour to a greater or lesser extent.

Sometimes we meet people who are obviously suffering from a recognisable mental illness. They are muttering to themselves and giving periodic whoops of joy. They have covered themselves with a blanket and sit huddled in a corner. They assure us, that they are really the President of the United States, or they constantly look back furtively, convinced that they are being followed by men from outer space. When we meet such people, it is not our responsibility to diagnose or cure them. If we can, we try to make their lives a little more pleasant, a little less stressful—even if it is just for a fleeting moment.

We must appreciate that whatever is wrong with them is as real and valid as a broken leg. The treatment they get, however, is often harsh and unsympathetic. This may be unfair but it is not surprising. Physically ill patients are almost always co-operative and grateful. Generally they do not get in the way. They stay where they are put which is right, proper and as it should be.

Mentally ill patients are often uncooperative, unpredictable, ridiiculously self-centred and heedless of the good advice and kind attention given to them. On top of that, they may be destructive and threatening. All this does not make them lovable. The unspoken argument often seems to be that if human beings behave in a sub-human manner, they will inevitably be treated a such.

There can be little doubt that the majority of mentally ill patients do not get the care and attention needed to diagnose and cure their condition to the same extent that would be theirs if they were physically ill. Of course, there are centres of excellence where everything possible is done for comfort and care and where the recovery rate is high. On the whole, however, most of us would prefer a fractured femur to a nervous breakdown.

The preceeding paragraphs highlight another disadvantage of the mentally ill. They immediately become 'they' while we are 'we'. The truth obviously is that they are 'us'. They are not a different breed. They are us when we have become the victims of a condition that affects our behaviour. No more, no less.

If people we know begin to act 'oddly' there is no reason for us to sheer off. They won't bite and it's not catching. It is silly to argue with them or to explain where they are wrong. When they are mentally ill, they have no choice. Just go along with them. Ease the tension. That is usually all you can do. And, for goodness sake, don't make fatuous remarks like 'Pull yourself together.'

Remember too that few patients who are mentally ill are 'completely out of their minds'. Most of them are aware that something is wrong with them but they cannot do anything about it. Whether they are at home or admitted to hospital for treatment, they still value friendship and kindness. Being rejected and isolated adds to their distress just when they have more than enough on their plates. Visits, letters, little attentions are always therapeutic. They make people feel good.

If one of our acquaintances has just spent some time in hospital for a 'nervous condition', he may want to talk about it or he may not. The choice must be his. Our object is to make him feel welcome and accepted again. His wife, girl friend, parents, children, may be worried. Perhaps we can lessen their tension. If we understand what is going on, then we might be able to find the right words and the right actions. Basically we must accept that all deviant behaviour is the result of a cause and not a choice.

Having said all this, one might add that if we ourselves

have been mentally ill or know that we are suffering from a
mental ailment, it is a very good idea, if we can, to try and
relieve the embarrassment and curiosity of others. Just
discussing the condition objectively is proof of normality.
And, glory be, how everybody does love normality.

GLOSSARY

There are a number of technical or semi-technical words
and terms which have become part of our daily
'psychiatric' vocabulary. Many of them are misunderstood
or half understood and this seems a good place to give simple
explanations. As with almost anything, there will be experts
who disagree and niggle. Let them. These are definitions
culled from recognised and respected authorities and,
what's more, they make practical sense.

Psychology is the science of the mind ie: of human behaviour
and thought.
Psychologist is a person working professionally in the field of
human behaviour and thought.
Psychiatry is the science that studies abnormal human be-
haviour and thought. It is a field of medicine.
Psychiatrist is a medically qualified specialist dealing with the
mental and emotional problems of his patients.
Psychoses is mental illness.
Phobia is an exaggerated or obsessive fear.
Manic-depressive is a patient suffering from a mental disorder
in which there are alternating periods of depression and
euphoria.
Euphoria condition of exaggerated well-being.
Paranoia is a condition in which the patient suffers from
delusions.
Psychosomatic illness is a condition presenting physical
symptoms originating in emotional or mental disturbance
rather than in organic disease.
Neuroses is commonly known as 'nerves'. The patient knows
that he/she is tense and giving exaggerated importance to

ordinary experiences but cannot control these feelings or thoughts.

Psychopath is one suffering from mental instability and immaturity, losing all balanced sense of consequences and also losing all sense of right and wrong.

Schizophrenia is a mental disease in which the patient is confused, incoherent, disorientated and suffering from delusions.

Psychoanalysis is a method of treating neuroses or psychoses based on the teachings of Sigmund Freud (1856-1939). 'The essence of this approach is the investigation of repressed or unconscious desires so that the patient can be made aware of the forces which are influencing his behaviour and thus be enabled to bring them under voluntary control.'

CHAPTER SEVENTEEN

The Autistic Child

It has often been said that the family with a handicapped child is a handicapped family. In no case is this more true that with the autistic child.

Autism is a label that is often used when the diagnostician cannot think of anything else to say. It covers a large pattern of non-communicating, deviant behaviour. Yet the true autistic child is fairly easy to spot. He is completely withdrawn within himself and will not relate to, or communicate with anybody. He is obsessive and unreasonable, he has no speech, or very little, and seems to have no desire to say anything to anybody. All his wants are urgent and he will lose his temper and become destructive if they are not met. He does not respond to affection or threats. He lives in a little world of his own and it is not a happy world.

He will often sit on the floor and bang his head. He is excessively neat and will place his shoes, knives and forks and all other objects in an ordered position and then arrange and re-arrange them a thousand times. If anything in the home or in his daily routine is altered, he will become deeply perturbed. A peculiar trait is that he tends to walk on his toes.

He may be good-looking, bright and gifted in many ways. He may be otherwise damaged—perhaps deaf, spastic or epileptic. It is heart-breaking to see a child being miserable, inflicting self-damage, able to find comfort in nobody and nothing. The parents stand there watching, wanting with every fibre of their being to help the child, but they cannot get close to him.

Almost all parents of autistic children can be heard, at some point, lamenting that if only their son or daughter were a Mongol, they would be able to love him or her and get love back. As it is, they get nothing but heart-ache. Therapists—medical, educational and psychological—have tried in all sorts of ways to break through the barrier with varying degrees of success. Improvement depends partly on the severity of the autism and partly on the efficacy of the treatment. Some of the children show little or just sporadic improvement. They become schizophrenic men and women. For some reason, one rarely hears reference to an autistic man or woman.

Most of the children gradually develop some responses. Reactions become less violent. Language is often mastered but it is usually fairly stiff and formalised. Human relationships are formed but they are rarely easy and ordinary. The child still lives on an island, comes over to the mainland for short visits and then returns. He is not at home outside himself.

It is ironic that the parents of the children who make the greatest progress, must often worry most about the future. Few severely autistic children ever reach that pinnacle of success where they are fully independent and self-sufficient. They may become socialised enough to be acceptable in a superficial way. They always remain 'outsiders' to a degree because their thought processes are not ordinary. They have a logic all their own. Their priorities are not ordinary. Their social reactions are strange. (We are not considering what is right or wrong, good or bad but just the fact that they are different.)

They seem to lack all subtlety or insight. They do not discriminate finer shades of meaning or feeling. There are the infinite number of little experiences which the ordinary person absorbs or learns automatically or coincidentally, which are completely over the heads of the autistic. Even when one of these lessons is carefully explained, it will be learned in a literal, one-off manner.

Where do these teenagers, and later adults, fit into our society? It is a gamble, with the odds still stacked against them, that they will find a residence and employment suitable to their needs and capabilities. The obsessive violent child who shows little or no improvement provides a problem that is fundamentally easier to solve if only we bothered to solve it. They need sanctuaries so that their families can be relieved of the burden of their presence—not only with a clear conscience but with the assurance of knowing that the sanctuary is right for the child. Most parents have a deep love and sense of responsibility for their autistic sons and daughters. Many have a sense of guilt. Since nobody can yet tell them why their child is that way, they feel it must be something they did that was wrong. They get little sympathy and the whole family may become socially unacceptable because the autistic child is unacceptable. Friends, neighbours, and relatives as well, feel they do not want to be involved or they feel that somehow they should be able to help. Because they can't, they become uncomfortable and stay away. So the family that is under the greatest possible stress and provocation, which desperately needs support if it is to survive as a unit, gets little or none.

Places for these seriously disturbed children, and help for their parents, should be a high priority. Until it is, a helping hand, an understanding pat on the shoulder are worth a lot. There is not much that can be done, casually, for the child himself if he happens to be highly disturbed.

On the other hand, when there has been improvement, when one can make contact, then a spot of friendship can go a long way. The adolescent or late teenager, who, at first, appears practically normal, but who has unusual reactions, who comes out with irrelevant remarks, whose use of language is pedantic, is an easy butt for ridicule. It may be difficult to assess how this affects the 'butt'. On the whole ridicule, sarcasm, wit are concepts that he cannot understand. One can observe, however, that when he is accepted and when he feels that he is participating, it gives him satisfaction.

Perhaps an acceptable definition of autism might be a deprivation of satisfaction. Here is ample room for at least a little compensation.

CHAPTER EIGHTEEN

Aphasia

People sometimes get mixed up when they hear talk about the autistic and the aphasic child. Both words start with 'a' and refer to non-communicating children. There the similarity ends. Oh, one could add that both conditions appear to be inborn and that they are often found in conjunction with other damage. But basically they are totally different. Autism is a mental illness that manifests itself in deviant behaviour whereas aphasia could almost be described as a mechanical hang-up.

The human brain has often been compared to a computer but for present purposes it would be more appropriate to liken it to a modern telephone exchange, highly sophisticated and yet things go wrong, wires get crossed, unwanted numbers come up, one cannot get through. Sometimes people just cannot make the cerebral connections which, normally, are no trouble at all.

If we want to say something, we say it. Sometimes we do not know exactly what to say and we hem and haw a bit and occassionally we blather and are surprised at the nonsense we are talking. Generally we are in charge. If we want to say 'hello' we say 'hello' and if we want to say 'rubbish', we say 'rubbish'. The connections are all there and they are working beautifully.

Some children—bright, otherwise ordinary children—cannot make this connection. They know what they want to say but it does not come out right. The part of the brain that is responsible for receiving orders and sending out the messages is not functioning properly.

If you understand what is wrong, you try to put it right. You either repair the system or you get another department of the telephone exchange to take over the job. You do not, if you have any efficiency whatsoever, leave it not working. Aphasic children have long been neglected and misunderstood. They cannot talk properly but that does not mean that they are silly, lazy or deaf (though, once again, they may be all three). We are dealing with an invisible handicap and, as usual, there is a lot of rejection, neglect and buck passing.

The kids often go through a bad time because they are misunderstood and frustrated. The very young aphasic child, like all other handicapped children, does not know that he is 'different'. He is himself. Fine. That is the way you accept him. Actually, if you were not told that he is thought to be aphasic, you would probably just say that he was a slow speaker and think no more about it. Because the word aphasic is used some people become uncertain of themselves. Forget it. You can make contact. You can do things together.

Generally, even if he cannot talk easily, he will be able to understand what you say. There is no reason why he should be stupid and if he is not stupid and you are friendly, he will soon be able to show you how you can get along together. He may, however, be retarded. Some children are. Accept him as he is. All that is needed is time, a little patience and lots of good will; they add up, if you like children, to a lot of fun.

As soon as his aphasia is diagnosed, his parents and teachers will be busy working to help him master his handicap. Unless you are specifically asked to 'work' with him, do not add to his stress but take him as he is and, in doing so, you will be relieving the parents of tension too. Each child, each family, is different and you will have to play it be ear.

This analogy of the telephone lines not making the right connection applies to other conditions as well. Sometimes children (or adults) have perfect hearing but the pattern of language which they hear is not received and decoded by the brain. Language as they hear it and as they would like to use it, does not make sense to them. They are dysphasic.

In other cases, the spoken word may come across loud

and clear and full of meaning. Speech may be perfect. When, however, language is written down, the pattern which the letters make has no significance and is meaningless and confusing. Writing is impossible or terribly difficult because the mind's eye cannot see the sense of peculiar squiggles. All writing is illegible to them. This inability to read or write is called dyslexia.

There is a strong social stigma attached to illiteracy. All people of average intelligence and education are expected to be able to read and write. This is something those who are dyslexic cannot do, or do badly. Therefore they are treated as unintelligent or lazy. They may be, but their dyslexia is another thing. It is a disability which makes life more difficult for them. You can make it easier by avoiding the written word. Don't write, telephone. If they cannot read, read for them. If they cannot write, write for them. They will probably be self-conscious about their trouble. They will need reassurance and building up by someone concentrating on all the things that they can do.

Once again experts disagree on what the conditions actually are and how best to deal with them. Constructive results have been obtained in a number of ways. The situation remains rotten when nobody is interested and nothing is done. But a lot can be done, if you decide it must be done.

CHAPTER NINETEEN

Strokes

In order to function properly, the brain requires a steady flow of blood. If the brain does not function properly the entire body and personality may be affected. Sometimes too much blood leaks into the brain. Sometimes a clot of blood stops the steady flow and the brain reacts violently. This is known as a stroke. Other terms used are CVA (cerebrovascular accident), cerebral haemorrhage, cerebral thrombosis, seizure, apoplexy.

The stroke may be so mild that it is not recognised as such. It may cause a fleeting loss of unconsciousness and interference with normal activity. It may be severe with prolonged unconsciousness leading to death. It may endure for several hours and when the patient returns to consciousness, he may be confused and unable to move normally. He may be incontinent. He may be unable to speak. It is literally a shattering experience. The brain has been damaged and the symptoms will be relative to the damage. With time the damage is usually completely or partially repaired and body functions are restored. This rarely happens overnight. There are days, weeks, months of despair and frustration.

Though the brain has been damaged, patients are often keenly aware of what has happened to them. They may be so paralyzed that there is no outward sign of understanding.

Many stroke victims have later spoken of the horror of lying there, unable to move at all, hearing doctors, nurses and, family discussing their plight and future. They have wanted to make some sign, any sign, that they were alive and conscious but all the connections were out of order. They were not in charge. They could not get through. Eventually, they might have been able to blink their eyes or move one finger. That was something. It was a beginning. At least they had one line open.

The speed and extent of recovery will depend on the severity of the damage, on the treatment and on the strength (in all senses) of the patient. He will need a great deal of encouragement and he is unlikely to get that if he is treated as a cabbage just because he is lying there like a cabbage. In spite of the stroke, he is still the person he always was. He may sound different. He may look and act different but that is the superficial manifestation of the condition.

Stroke victims are often left aphasic, at least temporarily. Then they suffer not only from the terrible frustration of being unable to say what they want to say, but they have the added burden of coping with people who look at them as if they were idiots. Even the best intentioned, well meaning folk can be thick as two planks when it comes to recognising the needs of those who cannot express themselves normally. There seens to be a comfortable conviction that if one smiles sweetly at some poor creature who is trying desperately and unsuccessfully to convey a message, that he should be happy whether the message has been understood or not.

If anybody is trying to tell you something and has difficulty in doing so, and you do not have the time or inclination to unravel it, simply say that you have to catch a train and clear out. You are entitled to do that. It is your choice. If, however, you are concerned and want to help, then do not let go until you have understood. The message may not be important in itself but it is important enough for the aphasic to warrant a big effort. Pencil and paper may help—either in spelling out whole words or in giving a choice of letters. Generally the easiest way is to ask the sort of questions that require a yes or no answer. How many questions are needed to hit the right answer depends upon your intelligence and ingenuity. It is the old parlour game put to good use.

Every time you leave somebody who has trouble expressing himself before you have reached an understanding, you leave him with a sense of failure. Every time you understand, you leave him with a sense of triumph and success and with the will to try again. This will to try again is probably the most important factor in the recovery of stroke victims.

We have mentioned the repair of damage but there is another theory that can be applied here. It is a theory or technique that works right across the whole field of disability, physical and mental. It is by no means new and really is just plain common sense. In simplest terms, it is the cliché, 'make the most of what there is.' Cliché or not, we do not all follow this advice. We could do any number of things far better than we do. Sportsmen and athletes prove this over and over again. They are ordinary people with ordinary bodies but they train their bodies to perform outstanding feats. Ballet dancers are born with ordinary feet but, in the course of time, by dint of hard work, they train their toes to take their full weight; they learn to balance on their points; they jump high in the air and land on those poor toes. If ordinary people tried to do the same they would land flat on their faces with bruised or broken toes as well. Those ballet toes have been taught to do things other toes cannot do. Proficient pianists have trained their fingers to cover the keyboard with incredible speed and accuracy. Good typists have done the same.

If we apply to the disabled our knowledge that practice does not only make perfect but makes the impossible possible we get some extraordinary and gratifying results. For example, we know that almost all deaf children have some residual hearing. We concentrate on that, exercise and manipulate it, raise it with hearing aids, and then practice, practice, practice. What happens? Children who are profoundly deaf learn to listen, learn to recognise the sounds that they do hear and begin to function like children with far, far better hearing. This is known as auditory training.

The same idea is applied to partially sighted children who are taught to make maximum use of whatever sight they may have. And what applies to children, is equally valid with adults.

We have learned a great deal from the way some of the

Thalidomide victims have adapted their damaged bodies to perform the actions which the able-bodied tackle quite differently. Not only do we train organs, limbs, senses, damaged or not, to work at their full potential but we train them to perform deeds that are not usually their domain. There is a very pretty young Thalidomide mother who was born without arms. She cuddles, baths, feeds and changes nappies with her legs and feet and she does it all with enormous competence. Ordinary mothers use their arms and hands. Since she has none, she has had to switch functions.

At this point, we can return to our stroke victims. Different parts of the brain are in control of different functions. If the part of the brain that controls speech is damaged by the stroke then, obviously, the patient's speech will be affected. Even while it is mending, the damaged brain can be stimulated and exercised. Furthermore, it is sometimes possible to divert or switch jobs from one part of the brain to another, just as it is possible to switch jobs from one limb to another or from one set of muscles to another. The possibilities are endless and where they have been explored, some of the results have been outstanding.

Victims of strokes have suffered a great shock. They are often sorely depressed. They are not fit and their energy is limited. It takes encouragement and outside enthusiasm to get them going again.

Many families are aware of this and husbands and wives, children and parents often dedicate themselves to the rehabilitation of the patient. They can use assistance. Some families, however, are unaware of the possibilities and an outsider can often open their eyes and give them and the patient new hope.

CHAPTER TWENTY

Spastics

Disabled people can be so tiresome. They even fuss about how they are labelled and talk about improving their image. Many spastics, for instance, prefer the term 'cerebral palsy'. Do they really think it will make a difference to the way they are treated? A rose is a rose is a rose. But just exactly what is this rose called cerebral palsy?

It is brain damage localised where it affects movement and posture. Again, because of the damage, connections cannot be made (see multiple sclerosis, strokes, Parkinson's disease). The spastic may want to tell his hand and arm to make certain movements but he is not in command. The hand and arm do not listen. They try to do their own thing. The damage is not hereditary. It may be the result of accident or disease but, more often than not, nobody knows why it happens. Yet it happens often. There are at least six spastic children born in Britain every day, that is over 2,000 each year. That is a lot of cerebral palsy.

Some of it is horribly severe. The victim may be totally immobilised, able to move only a finger or a left foot. (Have you read Christy Brown's *'My Left Foot'* *?) Speech may be impossible. Intelligence need not be affected; it may be extremely high—Christy Brown is an example of a brilliantly talented spastic who has written several best sellers. Brain damage may be more extensive and affect thought processes. It is also possible for the cerebral damage to be minimal and its only manifestion may be the slightest tremor of hands or feet. It is quite impossible to generalise.

Here are a few more definitions: Spastic or spasticity is stiffness of the muscles, interfering with movement and posture.

*Secker and Warburg 1972

Athetosis is a particular sort of uncontrollable movement and posture which interferes with the actual movement a person intends to make. (adjective = athetoid)

Ataxia is difficulty in co-ordinating movement (adjective = ataxic)

Hemiplegia is disability of one side of the body.

Paraplegia is disability of the legs only.

Quadriplegia is disability of all four limbs.

With spastics, we are concerned with three main sections of the brain: the cortex which is the outer layer and deals with thinking, moving and feeling, the basal ganglia and the cerebellum (see diagram on page 102). When the cortex is damaged, we have the basic condition for cerebral palsy. The child born with damaged cortex will have uncontrolled movements, muscle weakness and often interference with growth and development. It may affect all four limbs, or just those on one side of the body, or the legs only.

The basal ganglia and cerebellum are below the cortex and they control balance and co-ordination. When the basal ganglia has been attacked or has not developed properly, movements become graceless and uncontrolled. There is athetosis. That is why one sees some spastics strapped to their wheel-chairs. Otherwise they might be hurled out by the force of their own involuntary actions. Arms may flay about, heads jerk and there is great difficulty in speaking because of lack of muscle control. There may be grimacing. Even a laugh can sound weird. When the cerebellum is affected we tend to get ataxia.

The disadvantages of invisible handicaps have been discussed. Here we have the very opposite. Nothing is more visible that the effects of severe cerebral palsy. It is heartbreaking to see these poor children and adults. Is that really an advantage? Yes, if you are trying to collect funds for research, treatment, homes, schools, appliances. The public responds. It can see that these people are grossly disabled. At the same time, that is often all that the public does see. It looks no further. It turns its eyes away and refuses to look at the people concerned. It does not see them as human beings.

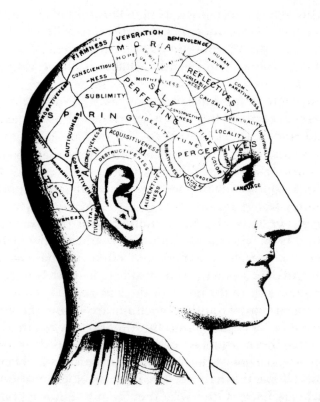

It rejects them. The discomfort of the disabled makes the able-bodied uncomfortable. It is easier to see all the severely spastic as mentally subnormal and therefore beneath our notice. There is often a communication problem. It would take time and trouble to surmount it. Who has the time? Who wants to take the trouble?

Many spastics complain that not enough is done to make the man in the street understand what cerebral palsy is. They have a naïve belief that if there were more understanding, there would be more acceptance. (This book is written under that conviction.) Realistically, there is a modicum of truth in the assumption but realistically, too, one must accept that life is hard for everybody and each person has only so much time for other people's troubles. The disabled, badly disabled, must learn that they are entitled to expect very little. If they wish to be accepted as ordinary people then they must learn about ordinary people and accept that ordinary people are generally self-concerned. They will accept only what is easily acceptable.

Here we reach a vicious circle. With perseverance, determination, specialised knowledge and ruthless exercising, it is possible to attain enormous improvement in the majority of spastic children. Most can be taught or conditioned to control many of their wanted and unwanted movements. It is not easy but it can be done. Intellectually, they can be stimulated and guided to use their intelligence to maximum effect—which is true of any child.

Unfortunately, too often the standards for these children are far too low. It is argued that life is hard enough for them without making it even more difficult. It would be cruel and wrong to expect too much. Anyway, what family or community has the resources to give a palsied child the dedicated attention that would be needed to get required improvement? It is kinder and more realistic to accept them as they are. But a severe spastic is not acceptable to society as he is, or, perhaps it would be more correct to say, a severe spastic is acceptable as a severe spastic, not as an ordinary person.

The severe spastic does not know what an ordinary person is. Few of these children as they grow into teenagers and adults are allowed relationships, even with members of their own families, that give them insight into the complexities of ordinary people and their lives. They, the disabled, see the able-bodied as a homogenous group for whom life is a piece of cake. They see themselves on the receiving end of very unfair treatment. True enough. What they are not shown is that fairness has nothing to do with life for anybody.

They do not see that they themselves are often grossly unfair. For instance, the majority, as they grow up, yearn for independence and often resent their parents' possessiveness and over-protection. This is natural, normal, ordinary. Few, however, have ever been given the chance to understand (or even feel that there is anything to understand) the emotional conflicts that beset their parents. Nobody can feel protective, responsible, hurt, worried for 15 to 25 years and then calmly say, 'Right. Over to you. I've done my bit.'

If a rose is a rose is a rose, so a son is a son is a son and a daughter is a daughter is a daughter. And what is more the sons and daughters are likely to have even bigger hang-ups than their parents. They must have because they are dependent, loving, grateful, resentful, frustrated, all in a jumble. Too often they cannot talk this out with anybody, probably least of all with their parents. This, of course, is further aggravated as they mature and sexual urges manifest themselves.

So much help is needed. This might be a good place to make a point that is relevant to any disability but seems to apply particularly to the spastic and the blind. There are kind men and women who devote much time and energy to helping their less fortunate fellow-creatures. In return they expect a certain amount of gratitude. They are offended when they do not get it. Instead of being paid for their services in hard cash at so much an hour, they want their payment in the form of thanks. It is a fine cold-blooded deal.

The disabled, apart from being normally courteous, may be willing to pay that price and say, 'Thank you. How kind. You are marvellous.' Or they may not. It is obvious impertinence to provide assistance that is conditional. You do it because you want to, or you don't do it. Also you do not inflict your 'kindness' where it may not be wanted. Obsessive do-gooders are a menace. Kindness may be appreciated or not. Nobody has a right to gratitude.

At the same time, the intelligent disabled person should be able to work out that the do-gooders who demand thanks are really just ordinary people wanting a little attention. They want to be told how good and important they are. They may have few other claims to fame. They need the dependence, respect, appreciation that the disabled might give them. They need it badly.

Once the disabled can understand that much about some of the able-bodied, then they may also have a better understanding of themselves and others like them. It may dawn on them that many of the disabled, though they demand to be treated as ordinary, actually need their disability to get attention and a sense of importance. If they were ordinary, nobody would look at them twice.

While we are on this tack (which may sound like woman's magazine mass philosophy but is fundamentally true and a truth that must be kept in mind) there are parents of disabled children whose lives would be much poorer if they did not get the sympathy and attention that having a disabled child brings them. This is not cynical. It is a recognition of the vulnerability of every human being. Each one needs reassurance and support and confirmation of his or her personal importance. Disabled or not, we are all vulnerable.

Too many sufferers from cerebral palsy are never encouraged to think these things out. It is a pity. Their lives are too sheltered and limited and they need to be taken out in every way. They want to see things, do things, discuss things. In practical terms there may be problems with wheel-chairs and access. These should not be insurmountable. Learning to manipulate a wheel-chair does not take much time or talent. Coping with practical problems like eating, drinking, going to the toilet may be new to the 'outsider' but will be routine to the disabled. It boils down to good will and the desire to communicate. Who needs more?

CHAPTER TWENTY-ONE

Parkinson's Disease

You sometimes see elderly people who shake uncontrollably, who walk with an unsteady gait and whose movements seem uncoordinated. Sometimes their feet appear to be glued to the ground and it makes them tilt forwards. They may have great difficulty in swallowing and talking. They are suffering from Parkinson's disease.

There is no known cause for the condition which is due to deterioration in a group of nerve cells in the basal ganglia of the brain (see diagram page 102). The disease rarely attacks young people but is prevalent among the over 60s. It was thought to be a localised ageing process but then it was found to be dependent on chemical changes.

The basal ganglia produces a substance called dopamine which, when functioning properly, it then absorbs. Without dopamine the nerves falling within the basal ganglia stop co-operating and do not work as they should. As with cerebral palsy, there is a lack of balance and uncontrolled movement.

In Parkinson's disease dopamine is not produced adequately. By swallowing a medicine called L-dopa, dopamine is again produced and normal functioning resumes. L-dopa or similar medication does not cure the condition but is an essential on-going treatment (like insulin in diabetes). So far the story is all roses but the drawback is that L-dopa may cause side effects which are undesirable. There may be nausea, vomiting, dizziness. The sense of taste is often affected. Patients may become moody, getting depressed or elated without due cause. They may be excitable and overactive. Their urine may be dark brown. This does not matter but is a bit disconcerting if unexpected.

All the side effects can be partially controlled by

regulating the amount of medication. The patient and medical adviser must work out the best formula. But despite optimum use of treatment, some of the basic effects of the disease may still be present such as stiffness, difficulty in moving and tremor. If general health deteriorates the effects of the condition become more evident, so it is important to see that the patient is as fit as possible and to make extra allowances when he has 'flu or a cold in the head. In the past (one hopes in the past) even the closest relatives were sometimes impatient with the clumsiness of sufferers and pleaded or demanded that they be a little more careful. This was understandable but unkind. On the whole will power is not a factor. Of course, if people let themselves go and make no effort at all, it does not help. On the other hand, it is more constructive to give a straw to woman who cannot hold a cup than tell her to stop shaking. At the same time it is a good idea for patients to carry on doing as much as they can for as long as they can. It does not help to molly-coddle them.

Muriel, an intelligent and once very attractive woman now in her early 70s, is fairly typical. With L-dopa, her palsy in under control but her movements are extremely slow. Her face and voice have lost almost all expression.

She spoke carefully, 'It is so stupid. I want to do so much and it takes me so long to do anything. If I drop my handkerchief, I can manage to pick it up eventually if nobody picks it up for me, but I get cross if they do not help me and even more cross if they don't let me do things for myself.' There was the ghost of a smile as she continued, 'Luckily I'm so slow nobody can wait to see my anger'.

As with cerebral palsy, strokes and some other disabilities, the most important thing to remember is that though there may be clumsiness, slurred speech and slow reactions generally, this does not mean that the intelligence, personality and humanity of the patient have stopped working. She does not like being the way she is. She did not ask to be that way. She had no choice and she does not want to be rejected and discounted just because a bunch of nerve cells in the basal ganglia have packed up.

CHAPTER TWENTY-TWO

Wheel-chairs

Wheel-chairs are great for people who cannot use their legs. Legs are more convenient; they are also more common. They are so common that, in ordinary life, little allowance is made for wheel-chair users. Most of us would find it quite impossible to invite one to our homes for a meal or a natter. There are stairs and no ramps or lifts. There is usually a clutter of furniture and it would be easier to entertain a horse.

Access to public buildings is improving a little but pubs, restaurants and many shops are still impossible.

It is a stupid situation. There are some very nice people in wheel-chairs, people whom we like as friends, whose company we enjoy. They vary, of course. Some are more delightful than others. There are many different reasons why they are in wheel-chairs. Some are children. Because of their disabilty, they cannot run about and chase each other or play hopscotch. They are still children and they want to have fun. A wheel-chair does not deprive them of their capacity to enjoy themselves. If they are deprived, it is because the entertainment is not provided. This is where the outsider comes in.

No kid in a wheel-chair wants sympathy or further reminders of his or her condition. They don't have to be reminded. They live with it all the time. They want to get away from it, to go places, see things and do things. A child in a wheel-chair is a cinch if you like children!

Adults in wheel-chairs are that and no more or less. Some of them are young and strong and play basketball or participate in strenuous sports. They may have broken their backs in accidents and their legs may now be useless, but otherwise they may be fine. There is bound to be resentment.

How much resentment depends upon them, individually, and is none of your business unless they want to share it with you. Take your cue from them.

Some wheel-chair users are almost completely paralyzed due to accidents or strokes. Some have cerebral palsy or multiple sclerosis. Others are old and frail. A few will have incapacitating conditions that cause constant pain. One can only watch and then decide what is needed, what can be given and what sort of human relationship can be formed. All that might be wanted is transport from one place to another.

Wheel-chairs are not as high or tall as most legs. The occupant therefore is always at a low level and gets a little weary of talking to other people's navels or getting a permanent crick in his neck. If you are going to have a conversation with somebody in a wheel-chair, get down to the same level. Pull up a chair if there is one available. If that is not easy, squat. Just remember that if you are not used to squatting or have not been doing your deep knee bends regularly, you make a pretty display of yourself trying to get up again.

If you are going to take a wheel-chair user out for a walk or shopping make certain that you know what you are doing. First of all, are you strong enough? Pushing a chair on the even surface of a room or corridor is one thing. Pushing on rough ground and manipulating kerbs is quite another. Wheel-chair users may be good-natured but they do not like being tipped out, bumped black and blue or scared out of their wits. They like going out but the price may be too high for them.

If you are pushing and the chair becomes stuck, do not force it. The rear wheels are likely to rise and the occupant may be spilled out. Back up and start again. Always push with two hands. It is the only way to have full control. If you use one hand only you may find yourself going round in circles.

Where possible, try to avoid kerbs but look for a ramp or slope. If the down kerb cannot be avoided, get a good grip,

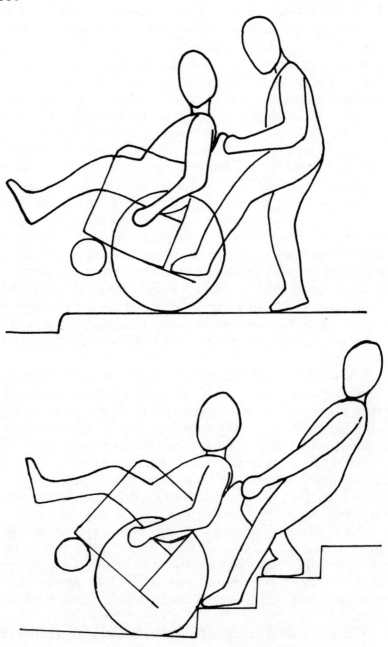

Going downstairs.

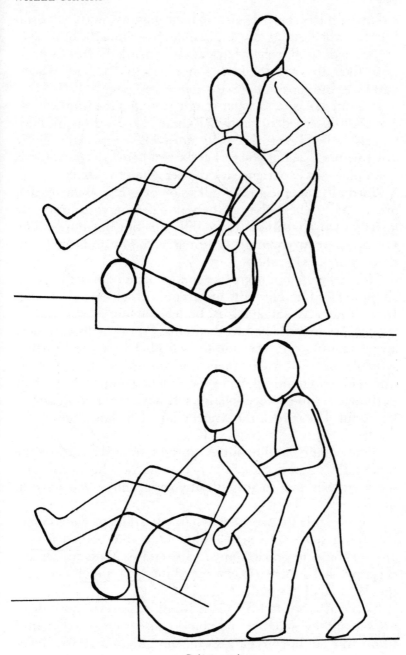

Going upstairs.

balance on the rear wheels, tip back slightly, and then drop
the rear wheels as gently as possible. Reaching the other side
of the road, tip the chair back again, raising the front wheels
until they are over the kerb. Then you lift the back wheels
and lever into position. (See drawings on pages 110/111).

It is much easier to cover rough ground if the front wheels
are slightly tilted up and the chair is driven on its back
wheels only. Try to keep off steep hills, especially going
downwards. Even if you feel certain of being in control, it is
not a pleasant experience for the person in the chair.

Normally, people go for walks side by side, talking to each
other. With wheel-chairs where one person is in front and
lower down chatting is more difficult, but not impossible.
Unless there are road drills or massed bands to deafen you,
there is no need to shout.

Most wheel-chair users like going out and doing their own
shopping and that literally means doing their own shopping.
It is in no way satisfying to be left outside stores while a
friend goes in and chooses the items. Woolworths and most
larger chain stores are fine for wheel-chair users but it is
sensible not to go at their busiest hours. It is almost
impossible to manipulate a shopping bag and a wheel-chair
at the same time. Wheel-chair users have laps and these can
be useful. Don't rock the wheel-chair. It is not a pram or a
cradle.

Before going out find out by straightforward questions the
toilet habits and needs of the person in the wheel-chair and
see how they can fit in with any programme you have in
mind.

It is possible to take wheel-chairs up stairs provided there
is enough space and man-power. One able-bodied person
alone should never attempt this exercise unless absolutely
certain of his or her strength and ability. It is much safer and
quicker to call in more help.

Never attempt to lift a chair by the arm rests since these
are usually detachable and could cause a nasty accident if
they came out in your hands while on a flight of stairs. Never
attempt to lift a chair by the foot rests either, since these also

usually detach. Instead, a good secure hold on the frame of the chair should always be adopted.

There are wheel-chair users who are frail, in pain or otherwise vulnerable. One meets their special needs. But, please, don't make the disabled feel that you are doing them a big favour. They probably are grateful and do not need you to tell them how good you are. Put the brakes on your ego and also do not forget that wheel-chairs have brakes too which are not only useful but essential when the chair is not moving. (All this advice comes direct from wheel-chair users.)

Incidentally, you may, at some point, be travelling by train and find yourself passing through the guard's van. There, huddled among the pigeons, mail bags and bicycles, you may spy a wheel-chair with a human being in it. Do not be surprised. It happens to be the way wheel-chair users are transported by rail in Great Britain. Extraordinary! They do not even guarantee delivery.

CHAPTER TWENTY-THREE

The Blind

Shut your eyes. You can't see. But you can open your eyes again. The blind can't. Ever. One can imagine what that is like and it is not pleasant.

Half shut your eyes and your vision will be altered. Even so, you cannot imagine what it must be like to be partially sighted. Yet the majority of those who are registered as blind have some sight. It may be very little but it is always better than nothing. There is absolutely no way for a stranger to know how much useful vision is there. Accept the person as blind even though of all the people you might see on the street with a white stick or guide dog 80 per cent will have some residual vision. It may mean that though they can see the number of an oncoming bus they will be unable to cross the street safely. This is understandable if one knows that their field of vision might be extremely limited. This field need not be in the centre of the eyes so that, in order to focus, the 'blind' person may have to look at things sideways. This often gives them a furtive, almost sly expression and many of them are aware of this. They complain that not only do they have the inconvenience of not seeing, but their social relationships are greatly hampered.

Whether we think of it or not, ordinary people depend a lot on eye to eye contact. We look into each other's faces. We look into each other's eyes and, rightly or wrongly, get a basic reassurance. Conversation with somebody who does not look at you is much more difficult. Looking people straight in the eyes carries conviction. Politicians and salesmen know this only too well. Blind people know it too but there is nothing they can do about it. And, of course, flirting becomes impossible. Few sighted people ever consider that point.

BRAILLE ALPHABET

A	B	C	D	E	F	G	H	I	J

K	L	M	N	O	P	Q	R	S	T

U	V	X	Y	Z	and	for	of	the	with

W	Oblique stroke	Numeral sign	Poetry sign	Apostrophe sign	Hyphen	Dash

Lower signs	,	;	:	.	!	( )	?	" "

The inability to flirt probably does not disturb the majority of blind people unduly, for 70 per cent of them are over 65 years old. Comparatively few children are born blind or lose their sight early in life. There are therefore not all that many special schools for them. When it comes to their education, there are the usual arguments for and against integration in ordinary schools.

The special schools can afford the newest, highly sophisticated and expensive technological aids. The teachers are specialised and highly skilled. On the other hand, these schools, in many ways, must inevitably be more sheltered and protective. There is no justifiable reason for academic standards to be lower but they often are. In these special schools there must be more experience of blind children and therefore there is more understanding and consideration. The children then often grow up expecting the same understanding and consideration from the outside world. Life is not like that.

Also schools for the blind automatically accept some of the habits and quirks that their children develop. Many of these

'blind behaviour characteristics', though not necessarily
offensive, are strange and so somewhat unacceptable to
ordinary people. Blind children who are integrated are soon
licked into conforming shape.

This controversial question of integration is common to
children with most disabilities. There may be many
advantages but they cannot exist if integration simply means
that the handicapped child is physically there. Unless he is
accepted in the fullest sense of the word, he might as well be
elsewhere. There can be no useful integration unless there is
participation. The youngster, complete with disability, must
be part of every activity. It may be hard because there is a
handicap, but the whole of life is more difficult for anybody
with a handicap. That is what the words means. He might as
well learn to put in that extra effort, to fight for his rights,
while he is young and has the support of parents, teachers,
class mates, rather than wait till he leaves school and has to
tackle the thoughtlessness and possible rejection of ordinary
life on his own.

In many ways, those who were born blind or went blind
early in life, have the edge over the blinded. They are usually
adept at Braille (page 115) and they have learned all the
tricks of the trade. They are mentally adjusted to their
disability. They are at home in their unseen world. Their
personalities and behaviour and approximation to the
standards of the sighted world will depend on their past
experiences, on their education in the fullest sense of the
word.

Those who lose their sight are really two people: those
they were originally and those they become. Naturally, the
way any disability is accepted or not accepted depends upon
each particular person. That is true regardless of the age at
which blindness occurs.

The ordinary man and woman has most encounters with
the blind in the street or in public places. There is the usual
classic situation of the blind wanting to cross the street. Do
you help or don't you? Find out. Ask them.

Rule one: make it clear that you are speaking to the blind

person. There may be a lot of sundry noises and many people talking. He will have no certainty that you are addressing him unless you make it clear. 'Hello. Do you want to get across? Need any help?' That is unambiguous.

You may be thanked and told that all is well, he can manage. Leave it. He may thank you and accept. The next question is, 'Do you want to take my arm?' Hold it out so he cannot miss it. The majority of blind people prefer to be led. There may be one or two who may ask you to take their arms. For goodness sake, don't grab them and push.

When you approach the kerb or steps, don't just say, 'Here is a step,' or 'two steps.' Say whether they are up or down. Many blind people have had nasty jolts when they expected steps to go up and they went down.

Going through doors, it may be impolite generally to push yourself ahead of people. When you are leading a blind person, always go first with his hand on your arm or your shoulder. Make certain that the door does not bang in his face or knock him down from behind.

If you are trying to direct him, make sure that your directions are concise. It is little use telling him that a chair is 'next to him'. Next to him is all the space around him. More and more blind people are becoming mobile and independent. They take buses. Conductors and passengers are often most solicitous but useless. 'There's a seat up front' does help a person who cannot see. He does not want to land on six strange laps before hitting the empty seat. Either lead him to the space or tell him its about four feet on the left.

He may be travelling by train and sit next to you in the dining car, or you may be at the same table in some restaurant. If he is independent enough to find himself in such situations, he will probably be able to get on by himself. You and he have nothing to lose if you ask whether he wants help. Buttering bread, for instance, remains a messy job for most blind people no matter how capable they may be. If he welcomes the suggestion, butter it for him and then take his hand and guide it to the plate where the bread and butter is. He may be grateful if you give him a clock description of the food on his plate. 'The potatoes are at eleven o'clock, the meat at six o'clock and the beans at two o'clock.' Telling him that the salt and pepper are in front of him is too vague. If he knows that they are at 12 o'clock, three inches from his plate with the salt on the left, he will be in the picture.

Among the constant problems that the blind have to tackle are toilets. It is not hard for them to ask where the Gents or the Ladies might be. But often they are taken there and then abandoned. Give them as much information as you can. Tell them exactly where the paper is, and most important, show them where the flushing handle is. Otherwise they may have to grope around for some time searching for the darned thing which might be hanging suspended from the ceiling, built into an adjoining wall or be a pedal on the floor.

Not surprisingly toilets are often easier for girls and women than they are for males. Almost everybody knows the story of the little girl on a country outing with her school who watches a boy relieving himself against a tree and remarks, 'That's a handy gadget for a picnic.' If you are a blind chap, aiming the gadget accurately is no picnic.

Let us stay out-of-doors with the blind for a bit. Some of them have guide dogs. There are ordinary men and women who have the most extraordinary misconceptions of the powers of guide dogs. Contrary to their beliefs, guide dogs do not read, write, or speak foreign languages. Basically their function is to prevent the blind from running into obstacles. The dogs do not tell their handlers when to cross the street. They are trained to sit and wait until the handler gives the instruction to cross. Here the handler may appreciate outside assistance. It is the handler, who is in charge.

This story must be true because so many blind people tell it. It's about the lady in the street who was asked by a blind man for directions to a certain shop. She bent down and carefully explained to the guide dog that he was to take the third turning on the left, then the second on the right and it was the shop next to the corner. He could not miss it.

It is not very often that one meets older blind men and

women alone on the street. At their time of life, they are not looking for challenges. Few of their needs or desires are urgent enough to force them out alone. They do not want to be old and blind. They are fed up or resigned. They badly need company and they badly need help. Even in a welfare state, there are not enough social workers for the blind. There are too few social workers generally. Volunteer organisations and good neighbours must step in and take on the responsibility of helping with shopping, cleaning, mending, cooking and similar chores.

When you go to the home of a blind person, perhaps with some shopping that you have brought, do remember elementary rules. Don't move furniture or other objects even if you think they would look better or be more convenient elsewhere. Don't leave doors half open. More noses have been broken by half open doors than than by all the boxers who ever stepped into a ring. If you have been shopping, tell the blind person exactly what there is and where it is. A blind person cannot tell a tin of soup from a tin of peaches until he has opened them. Tell him that you have put a rubber band round the fruit and he won't make a mistake. You might also make sure that you have not neatly put his tin opener where he can't find it.

The elderly blind need somebody to read and write their letters and attend to their bills and—guess what? Treat them like human beings. Radios and talking books are all marvellous but they don't talk back. You cannot exchange ideas with a broadcaster. Many of the elderly blind are very lonely. Many of them talk too much when they get a chance. Who can blame them?

Incidentally, the blind themselves often feel that they talk too much or talk out of turn. They reckon it's because they cannot see the ordinary necessary signals that normally denote that a conversation is finished or that a new topic is due. Again, one of the problems is that they do not know when people are talking to them. A question hits them from somewhere but it may be directed at a person nearby. The blind man has no way of knowing unless his name is used or there is some other clue like a tap on the arm. There must be identification.

Talking of identification, almost without exception, blind people, young and old, express a desire to strangle all the wits who accost them and chuckle, 'Ho,ho. Bet you can't guess who this is.' It is a joke that has worn thin many years ago.

This does not mean that they do not value friendliness. Too often, they hear somebody say, 'Saw you the other day but didn't stop. Was on the other side of the street,' or 'catching a train,' or some other excuse. On the subject of friendliness and sociability, blind men have a much easier time than blind girls or women. More of them get married. This would be in the nature of things. Caring and mothering is still inherent in most women. They think little or nothing of marrying a blind man with the main object of getting satisfaction from looking after him.

Men, as long as they are neat and clean and 'properly' dressed, are acceptable. It is deplorable, but women are still expected to be attractive and it is very hard for a woman who is blind to dress as smartly as her sighted counterpart. She cannot know if her lipstick is on straight and if it is the most flattering colour or if her skirt is the current fashionable length. Blind girls may be admirable but they are rarely chased. (And if a blind reader should be getting this from a talking book, that last word is spelled C H A S E D.)

Probably the blind person's best friend is the telephone. using it, they are at no disadvantage whatsoever. If you know any blind people, whenever you have a free minute, give them a ring and have a chat. You'll enjoy it.

CHAPTER TWENTY-FOUR

Diabetes

Diabetes is a condition where there is too much sugar in the blood. The patient is treated with insulin and then all is well. That sounds simple enough. Why have diabetes in a book about disabilities, real disabilities?

Diabetes is not simple. There are a number of misconceptions. There is much ignorance and prejudice and it can do nobody any harm to know just a little bit more about it.

First of all, let us consider the condition itself. All the cells in the body require glucose to keep them going. A car needs petrol; cells need glucose no matter where they are and what their function. Insulin is a hormone produced in a part of the pancreas (a gland which lies behind the stomach) which has the ability to turn sugar into glucose so that it can be used by the cells. If the insulin is not produced naturally then there will be too much unprocessed sugar. This produces the symptoms of diabetes which are thirst, loss of weight and energy and passing a large quantity of urine. There may be other symptoms as all parts of the body will be crying out for their fuel. When they are deprived, there will be many reactions depending upon the muscles, nerves or organs particularly affected. Diabetes has therefore been called not a disease but a syndrome, a pattern of different symptoms.

If the diabetes is not diagnosed and treated, the results can be fatal. The condition can be found in children or it can develop later in life. The diabetic child can usually learn to adjust to insulin injections quite easily and quickly. There is also a special diet and special times for eating and this can be a tremendous bore for any youngster. Parents must supervise the child's eating habits carefully until they are certain of his or her own sense of responsibility.

With a balanced intake of insulin and a controlled diet,

the child will be like any other child and be able to go to
ordinary school, competing with all other children on equal
terms academically, athletically and socially. No problem at
all except that proviso of balanced intake of insulin and
controlled diet. With the best will in the world, this is
sometimes difficult to maintain consistently and constantly.
There is no known cure for diabetes. The treatment is all
important.

There are times and situations when the child's body
reacts differently to insulin injection and to food. These may
be outside factors like climatic or geographical changes, or
they may be emotional tensions. They may be the physical
changes that go with strenuous exercise or they may be due
to a bug like 'flu or a cold. All these may have an effect on the
child's reaction and must be watched carefully.

Ordinarily a diabetic boy or girl in a classroom is no extra
trouble at all but the teacher must be aware of the possibilities. The child may show signs of having too little sugar
in the blood. Natural insulin automatically regulates itself.
Injected insulin continues lowering blood sugar until food is
taken to restore balance. Because of this continued action of
the injected insulin, meals are needed at regular intervals or
the blood sugar level falls too low bringing about a condition
called hypoglycaemia. The child sweats and becomes
drowsy, pale, absentminded and stubborn. He may find it
hard to talk or read. He may cry for no reason. There may be
complaints about tummy ache and pins and needles. There
may be vomiting and faintness. The child needs sugar or
carbohydrates quickly. Glucose sweets should be kept
handy. Biscuits or a sandwich will put things right. Most
teachers rightly object to pupils sucking sweets during
lessons, but allowance might be made for a diabetic child.

There is another important area in which an awareness of
diabetes would be desirable. All disabled children tend to be
labelled and once they are labelled, that is what they are
considered to be. Occasionally they may suffer from more
than one easily discernible handicap and they are then
labelled multiply-handicapped. On the whole, if a child is

known to be blind or partially sighted or hearing impaired or mentally retarded, he is accepted and treated as such. Few diagnosticians tend to look further once they have established what the main condition is. The possibility of diabetes in an already otherwise handicapped child is often overlooked. The child may appear dull or uncooperative or generally difficult. It is not unknown by any means for the otherwise disabled kid to have to pass out and go into a diabetic coma before anybody has the bright idea to test him for diabetes.

Of course, this is scandalous and bad paediatric practice, but most doctors are overworked and even in multidisciplinary assessment centres diagnosis is not always as comprehensive as might be desired. Doctors do not see their young patients often or long enough to be made aware of all their symptoms. The people who almost always know their child better than anybody else are the parents. Only a small proportion of parents are medically trained but that does not mean that they are unobservant. If they are alert to the possible implications of their observations, they can be invaluable in guiding their medical practitioners to a complete and correct diagnosis.

Diabetic children must almost always depend on insulin injections which many of them learn to administer themselves from a surprisingly early age. Adults who develop the condition later in life are often able to regulate the sugar content with pills taken orally. Their diet must be controlled and then there will be little or no trouble. There are diabetics who are outstanding in business, sport, show business, politics. As long as their insulin supply is correctly controlled they are fine.

Again, there is no absolutely reliable way of knowing how each individual patient will react under varying conditions. They must be prepared all the time for any eventuality. Insurance companies are aware of this. Many do not like insuring diabetics. They think it might be too much of a gamble. They ask for higher premiums. Large companies, the Services (armed and civil), are sometimes chary of employing men and women whose insurance premiums are above the normal. They too wonder just exactly what they are taking on. There is a generally unmentioned prejudice which diabetics have to fight all along the employment line. To avoid this prejudice, they often prefer not to mention their diabetes. They keep it quiet. Nobody knows about it. They may find it impossible to avoid meals and meal times that are utterly unsuitable for them. When they react badly, nobody knows what is wrong and nobody knows what to do. It is a stupid vicious circle.

When diabetes gets out of control, it can be very unpleasant. Even today when knowledge of its potential nastiness plus knowledge of how to tame it is so widespread, it remains one of the most prevalent causes of blindness in the elderly. About 80 per cent of patients who have suffered from diabetes for more than 20 years have eye lesions. In the vast majority of cases these will not interfere unduly with vision and even if left untreated, will cause blindness in only about 10 per cent of the sufferers. The danger is not great but is more noticeable today than it was 20 or 30 years ago when most diabetics died younger and one therefore did not meet the older ones whose sight was affected.

Some heart conditions are attributable to diabetes.

Very much on the credit side of medical progress is the present ability of diabetic women to produce normal healthy babies. The effect of maternal diabetes on the unborn child can now be monitored and corrected. In the past, most of the babies were abnormally large and were therefore delivered by Caesarean operation. Now the foetal weight can be controlled too and the mother (and baby) enjoy normal delivery.

Much of ordinary life is walking a tight rope of one kind or another. We have to learn to keep our balance. All diabetics are very much poised on that rope, not only in controlling the balance of their insulin in-take but also in balancing the image which their condition has with the public. They want to be accepted as ordinary and they are entitled to that acceptance but they also want the public to be aware of the possible consequences of their condition. It is hard to know what to do to get a balanced reaction from the man in the street.

Though there is some ignorance and economic prejudice, diabetics are lucky in that their handicap is 'socially acceptable'. There is no stigma. They look and act like other people. There need be no hang-up in discussing pros and cons with friends and neighbours.

If they are coming to visit you, find out what the most acceptable foods are. Nothing special will be needed, just the right choice. Too much alcohol is to be avoided but adults can enjoy a drink or two in safety. The diabetic may need food more urgently. Don't stick to your rigid time table or wait for other guests who may be delayed. Meet his needs. If you are entertaining a diabetic child, the parents will always gladly put you in the picture as to what he can and cannot eat. With a little advice and a spot of common sense it all becomes a piece of cake which the diabetic can safely enjoy.

CHAPTER TWENTY-FIVE

Sex

If a man had an accident and broke his leg, it would be very surprising if this permanently affected his sexual urge. If the accident was more serious and he lost his leg, it would still be surprising if his sexual drive was affected. If the accident was even worse and he lost both his legs, there is no reason to suppose that this would necessarily interfere with his 'manhood'.

Before the accident, he may have been very strongly sexed or comparatively disinterested. He may have been expert or ignorant, kinky or conventional. Men and women vary enormously and what is normal for one is abnormal for another. And this is true whether they are able-bodied or not. It is also true whether the disability is acquired or congenital.

The whole world, these days, is conditioned by films, television and advertisements to see sex and romance mainly in terms of youth, good looks and fitness. The fact that sex is universal and covers all ages and all types is ignored. The disabled or infirm are expected not to shatter our romantic illusions and not to offend our aesthetic susceptibilities. Too bad.

The truth is that the sexuality of any individual depends not on his or her appearance but on physical and emotional make-up and life experiences. The personality and emotional maturity determine how the sexuality is directed. A healthy, energetic body will probably have more sexual drive than an older, frailer one, or one weakened by disability. The opportunities for love affairs and experimentation are fewer for the handicapped with their more restricted social lives.

Even when the physical condition of the disabled seems to preclude any possibility of ordinary sexual fulfilment, it should be remembered that the urge or drive is in no way correlated to the ability to express it.

The whole area is still a mine field to be crossed with the greatest care. Our present so called permissive society has made almost any sexual activity or attitude a socially acceptable topic of conversation. Beneath the chatter, there still lie hidden many of the hang-ups and confusions which existed previously.

Many parents and children still find it hard to communicate whether there is a disability or not. When the disability is actually one of communication as with the deaf, sex is often covered with a short list of 'do's and 'don'ts' which may be simple and straightforward but are unrelated to actual human behaviour.

Parents of healthy, tough, mentally sub-normal teenagers are faced with a big problem and they know that there is no simple solution. The teenager in a wheel-chair will probably not want to discuss his sexual thoughts and feelings with the parents on whom he is dependent and to whom he is devoted. He will not want to add to their burden and also like any other teenager, he needs some privacy.

A comparative stranger who is sympathetic may easily find himself involved in the more intimate problems of the disabled and their families.

If you happen to be that stranger, or even a close friend, the help given must depend on your own experiences and attitudes. How you feel will naturally colour whatever you say or do. You may be shocked; you may be fascinated, attracted, roused; you may take it all in your stride. You may decide to do something about it yourself. The choice is yours. Whether you get involved at all or how far you get involved is up to you.

This is meant to be a practical book. For example: how does one help a blind person across the street or how is a wheel-chair manipulated at a high kerb? No great problems there. Sex, however, as mentioned before, is a highly emotional subject and requires a strong sense of responsibility. In some cases, helping the disabled to achieve an orgasm may be the right answer. It may also be an introduction to unwanted and impossible emotional demands. Hand and body play may give pleasure and a satisfying measure of fulfilment. It may also lead to a quite unwarranted degree of guilt. It is also by no means unusual for a person who forms a relationship with a disabled partner to become over possessive. This may be resented by the disabled and rejection may follow causing much pain.

The disabled, on the whole, are used to pain both physical and emotional. The able-bodied often are not and therefore when they are on the receiving end of rejection, it hurts all the more.

There are now quite a number of books and booklets available on sex and the disabled, and some cities have sexual centres. Parents of disabled teenagers and the disabled themselves should make use of them. They are honest, practical and helpful.

What must be remembered is that infirmity, physical disability, old age, do not automatically ban sexual interests and urges. One must accept that they are there and that they vary just as much as among the able-bodied.

On a slightly lighter but nevertheless valid level: flirting seems to be out of fashion at present. The general permissiveness which allows men and women to get to grips without many preliminaries, has put an end to the delights of word and eye play. Aggresive woman's libbers would probably snarl at the idea of flirting and many men don't seem to know what the word means. That is sad for flirting can still be a most pleasant, harmless pastime doing the egos of flirters a world of good. That too includes the disabled.

CHAPTER TWENTY-SIX

Bereavement

What should one say to a widow? What can one say to parents who have lost a son or daughter? How can one comfort a child who has lost its mother? How can one try to explain or justify an unwanted death? Is there anything one could do to help?

There can be no rules for behaviour, no book of set instructions which ensure instant comfort. Death, in many western communities, is still the one big unmentionable. There was a time when sex was not discussed. The word cancer was never mentioned. Death has taken over. Most of our attitudes are still very primitive. Death is the Grim Reaper and if we do not mention him, perhaps he will go away.

A few sincere believers have no doubt of an after-life. For them death is just a passing over. Be that as it may, for those who are left behind, it is usually a final farewell, the ultimate loss. There are many different ways of reacting to the loss, depending on the individual and the situation. The pain, distress and confusion can be completely unsettling and crippling.

Here our society behaves in an unexpected way. It *expects* the bereaved to be more or less disabled by grief. There is actually a perceptible amount of shock and slight disapproval if bereavement is met without undue emotion. What have we here? A cold fish? Deplorable! Death is fearful and fearsome and should be treated as such. Our society seems to have more respect for death than it does for life, more respect for the dead than for the living. The whole attitude is barbaric and what is more, it is impractical in a practical age.

Grief, disabling grief, is accepted as the inevitable price of death. The fact is that grief is an illness, an indisposition of the entire person and if the condition is not analyzed and understood, it cannot be treated. We take refuge in the fact that with time, grief heals itself. That could be said of many complaints but is is not usual medical practice just to let nature take its course, with little thought to alleviating pain and discomfort.

Dr. Colin Murray Parkes in his book, *'Bereavement'*, carefully observes reactions to bereavement in a large sample of the population, and charts the usual course that grief takes. He analyzes its manifestations, and reports on the many psychosomatic conditions that can result. There are clear cut patterns of behaviour. Reliable prognoses can be made.

Dr. Parkes writes at length, and with the understanding that comes from educated observation, of the pain, fear, searching, anger and even guilt that seem inevitable with the loss of a loved one.

Let us give bereavement and its consequences a closer look. It is unlikely that any human being can go through life without bereavement at some point or another. In the natural scheme of things most parents die before their children. We are the next generation. It can be a very sad loss when a mother or father dies. Here, obviously, one of the most relevant points is the age of the offspring.

A baby will not notice if Daddy suddenly disappears. A baby will cry for his mother but a surrogate mother who fulfils his needs for food, comfort and love will usually find a quick acceptance. There may have been an initial bonding but there has not been enough time for the development of emotional ties as adults define them.

A man of 50 may be sad when his 80 year old father dies but he is unlikely to be disabled by the event. He may see his father as a fine old man who played a determining role in his life and to whom he will always be linked by bonds of

Bereavement by Dr Colin Murray Parkes
Pelican Books, first published 1972

affection and gratitude. The death will mean a loss but it is an acceptable situation.

An 8, 12, or 15 year old boy may be completely un-balanced by the death of a father who is the keystone of his existence. Losing the strength, support and friendship of one so close at a vulnerable age may be unbearable. The strength, support, friendship will be fundamentally missed. It cannot easily be replaced. Attempts at replacement may be resented.

Slowly a pattern emerges. It is not the death of the person that matters. It is the loss of what that person's presence represented. It is clear that the death of a loved one who is far away is easier to take than the death of someone who is physically closer. Daily life is unlikely to be interrupted by the death of somebody who is not there anyway. During wars, women who lose their husbands on active service are generally able to cope with their loss. This in no way implies less love or devotion, but they have learned to live their daily lives apart from their husbands and therefore are not com-pletely lost. Somehow they can manage.

If we consider the many cases where adults live with their ageing parents, we will see that a mode of living will have become established. There may be friction, resentment, lack of freedom, extra unwanted work, exasperation. All these may form part of the picture but there is a pattern of living to which all have become accustomed. There is safety and comfort in habit. If the aged parent dies, even though it may be a blessed release for all concerned, there may also be genuine grief at the loss. It is not hypocritical. It is real but it is grief at the loss of the emotional security that existed, not grief at the death of the person. This is despite any true affection that may exist.

Now let us look at widowhood. There are more widows than widowers because men tend to marry women younger than themselves and women tend to live longer than men. A husband is a part of a wife. Without a husband, she is no wife. If he dies, part of her dies. The wife part of her is finished. That is shocking. Shock treatment is needed:

Warmth, quiet and tender, loving care. One often hears widows complain that since their husbands died, they are no longer treated as themselves. They are rarely invited out, even by old friends. Nobody ever bothers to explain to widows that they are no longer what they were. They are new and different people. They may not want it. They may hate it. If they have any common sense, they will face their renaissance as a challenge. At the time of widowhood, however, there is usually little opportunity for common sense to make itself felt. The emotions are overwhelming. They are called grief, grief for the person who has died. Actually they might more correctly be seen as despair at the loss that the death signifies.

Despite women's emancipation and liberation the majority of older women who lose their husbands have been home makers who have left many of the responsibilities of their lives to their husbands. Husbands still, on the whole, are the bread-winners. They are the investors and managers. They fill out the income tax returns and attend to major expenditure. The wives have their domain, the men theirs. It works out well until widowhood. Then there is often immediate panic.

There is companionship in marriage. People need each other. They need to reassure each other and share worries. If one dies, the companionship is gone. Women have responsibilities within a marriage. These responsibilities give meaning to their lives. Here lies their own importance. With the death of a husband, there are sometimes no responsibilities left and therefore no meaning. There may, however, be too many responsibilities. How can a woman bring up young children, run a home and earn the family's living all on her own? It is too much.

In many, many cases, the death of a husband on top of everything else also means a much lower economic standard. Being alone and poor is no fun. The grief is great. Again it is not basically the death of the person, but rather the results of that death which determine the emotional state of widows. It is not suggested that if all women had their own incomes, interests and independence from their mates, there would be no grief. Love and real companionship, friendship, complete understanding between a man and a woman will, one hopes, always exist. When death breaks up such a strong bond, there will be agony, real grief. This will not be confused with the desperation of finding one's place in what is left.

For the practical purposes of those who care to help the disabled, it seems essential to look at any situation that arises where there is bereavement and then work out what is causing the symptoms of grief. Only then can those symptoms be treated effectively. A widow who is used to the company of her husband will not appreciate being left by herself. It will only underline her loneliness. She will not want to face the ordeal of removing her husband's possessions on her own—having to do this will only stress her present frightening state. She needs a helping hand, somebody to talk to. She wants the assurance that somebody, anybody, will help her with the mortgage, the funeral, the car, taxes, whatever it is that is strange and frightens her.

Younger widowers are, on the whole, better able to cope with the pain of losing their wives, mainly because, apart from the ache of losing somebody whom they loved, they are self-sufficient. They may have relied on their wives in a million ways yet, fundamentally, men are usually trained to rely on themselves. The rules are deeply ingrained. They know how to cope. For many wives, being a wife is a profession. This is rarely true of husbands.

For the older man, the death of his wife can be more devastating. He has learned to depend on her. He is used to living in the comfort and security of her care. They may or may not like each other but they are used to each other. They feel safe with each other even if they bicker. He is deeply shaken when the security of his life with her is shattered. His grief can be helped enormously if there is some practical approach to the provision of his meals, laundry etc. Companionship may be more difficult to replace, but it is worth a try. Again the 'outsider' will not know what help to give until he understands what is upsetting the widower most.

The death of a child is a different matter. Dr. Philip Bloom (yes, he is related) in *'Grief is Important'*, an article in (Family Doctor) wrote, 'A parent's attitude to his or her child is often not fully appreciated. There is love, but what is love? It is a warm protectiveness towards something young, dependent, vulnerable and strangely appealing by virtue of being young. Children need their parents and this need gives the men and women who are parents a strong reason for their own lives; it fulfils them. It is a source of their own importance. It builds them up. Their children's need gives them strength and inner security. The death of a child shatters the very foundations of a mother's or father's emotional well-being. It must. The grief involved depends upon the depth of the feeling involved.'

He then goes on to deplore that mourning, formal mourning, has gone out of fashion in our society. It is a pity, for though much of it was formalised and meaningless, it did provide an outlet for otherwise inexpressible feelings. It was, in a way, official permission to grieve.

A word here about stillbirths: the importance of a baby who is born dead is often under-estimated. The body is often disposed of as though it were something negligible. After all, the child never lived. But for months, this baby was an important part of the mother (and father). It had great significance, actual and potential. Suddenly there is deprivation of all that significance. There is real grief and it should be respected.

All bereavement hurts to a greater or lesser extent, if only because it is a reminder of one's own mortality. Some bereavements hurt more than others. Civilised people will always try to comfort those in pain. They will try to alleviate the ache. Often much can be done to ease the situation. Sometimes one can only offer a sympathetic hand.

CHAPTER TWENTY-SEVEN

Chronic pain

For those who live with it, pain, physical pain, seems to have an existence of its own. It is a ruthless, bullying tyrant tormenting and toying with the victim. Sometimes it allows a blessed respite, only to return and once more clutch the body in its merciless grasp. Those who have lived with pain for some time, often say that they have learned to come to terms with it. They go along as it commands, try to ride on its back. This is usually a total effort and leaves them exhausted and empty.

The majority of disabilities, no matter how incapacitating, are physically more or less painless, but in the course of a lifetime, almost everybody meets someone who is suffering badly. Advanced stages of multiple sclerosis and cancer can be excruciating. The alleviation of intolerable pain is the domain of the doctor and the nurse. It is unusual for an outsider to be allowed to intrude. There may be some conflict here, for though the patients may want to be left alone to suffer in comparative peace they also have a deep need for understanding and diversion. They often want to talk to somebody. They are alone with pain too much.

If you enter the scene, just take it easy. Relax and try to offer what they want. Very often a friendly quiet account of what is going on outside, gossip about mutual friends, chatter about television personalities or programmes, politics or whatever their interests may be, will flow over them like soothing milk. You may get a response or not. Remember that you really cannot compete with pain. On a less acute but still thoroughly unpleasant level, it is almost certain that we will know people suffering from chronically painful conditions such as rheumatism or arthritis or back troubles like the ubiquitous slipped disc. There will be little or nothing that can be done to alleviate the agony but there is much that can be done to make life a little easier or more comfortable.

There are obvious things that one does not do. One does not shake hands energetically with somebody whose fingers are swollen and misshapen from arthritis. One does not warmly embrace anybody with a bad back. One does not grab the rheumatic elbow of a sufferer with the object of helping him across the street.

Betty, an attractive, efficient, successful social administrator in her early 50s was forced to retire because of her arthritic joints. She jotted down a few of her thoughts and they probably are all that need to be said here.

'The pain associated with arthritis is akin to having continuous toothache in your limbs, lessening at time but never leaving you. Don't keep on asking 'How are you?' because if the reply was truthful you would get fed up with 'I am in such pain' . . . .

Don't assume that if a person is no longer completely mobile that you must visit them at home. This attitude soon makes the arthritic house bound. If possible, and it usually is, issue an invitation to your home. If there are difficulties, overcome them. The arthritic will soon mention any seemingly insurmountable problems. The change of scenery will work wonders.

Don't offer to do the shopping if there is the slightest chance of the arthritic doing it. Offer to go along and carry the shopping.

Don't think that now Mrs X can only walk slowly and painfully that you cannot walk with her. Adapt your pace.

Remember that daily life for an arthritic demands a great deal of effort. Normal activities take on Mount Everest proportions. There is frustration at inability to cope fully, and depression from the continuous pain and fear of the future. Support, encourage and endeavour to understand.'

CHAPTER TWENTY-EIGHT

Something Wrong

When this book was first conceived, the plan was to treat each disability in three parts: the medical condition itself; the way it affects patients; what the man in the street can do about it. This seemed a sensible, balanced, objective approach. The only trouble turned out to be that it did not work. Though there were similarities and common patterns among certain often quite unrelated conditions, the differences were often basic and total. It would have been possible, but totally wrong, to deal with epilepsy and Thalidomide victims in the same way. Blindness and deafness, though often mentioned in the same breath, cannot be compared. They do not follow parallel lines. They are cast from different moulds. They must be handled differently.

Once it was recognised that the 'personality' of each disability had to be respected, then the trouble really started. As soon as the approach to each disability was not rigidly restricted, then judgement had to come into it and that, of course, is always precarious. How right or wrong the judgement turned out to be must be assessed by the reader.

The reason for this preamble is to explain and possibly justify why certain common, often devastating disabilities have had little space alloted to them while others, more obscure and less serious, have merited more attention. Some disorders do not need explaining. Their effects are either plainly understandable or wholly inexplicable. Every outsider knows where he stands, what he can and cannot do.

Heart conditions are often dangerous and uncomfortable. Chronic bronchitis, asthma, hay fever, emphysema can be agonising. There is nothing, however, that the man in the street could be told that would make him behave in any way that is more acceptable to the sufferer. The same applies to

the unfortunate people who suffer from allergies reacting
strongly and badly to normally acceptable stimuli such as
fur, feathers, dust, fruit etc.

It was puzzling to decide how to deal with people who had
laryngectomies (removal of voice box) or who stammered—
two totally dissimilar communication problems. At this
point, it really looked like insulting the intelligence of that
'man in the street' to give special obvious advice. Then we
reached the many people who can see and hear and think
normally, who can go anywhere and do anything, but who
are suffering, often profoundly, from something that is not
right. If we give obesity as our first example, somebody will
point out that extreme obesity prevents movement. Forget
about that. Just think of the average fat person. Often they
are miserable. Perhaps if they ate less and took more
exercise, they would lose weight. It may be that they are
suffering from glandular conditions that prevent them from
being slimmer. That is not our concern. The fact is that they
are fat and frequently unhappy.

Anorexia nervosa where people cannot eat and become
emaciated is the opposite of obesity. Others do not suffer
from that condition but are so naturally skinny as to be ugly.
There are people who suffer from alopecia, a disease that
makes them lose all or most of their hair. Perhaps this is not
as devastating for a man as it is for a woman. Nevertheless it
makes all its victims painfully self-conscious. Some babies
are born with large scarlet birth marks. Often these are on
their faces where they cannot be hidden. They go through
life branded. Others are the victims of fires or accidents that
leave them grossly disfigured. There are skin diseases such
as severe eczema which can be aesthetically unacceptable.
These are all visible physical disabilities.

There are other disabilities which are hidden but can
complicate life enormously. The Gay Liberation movement
may be growing and society generally may be more tolerant.
But homosexuals, male and female, no matter how much
they argue otherwise, are still suffering from a considerable
handicap. Sexually impotent men and frigid women may or

may not discuss their condition but they are all disabled to a degree. There are any number of unusual obsessions that can mar people's lives.

It does not lie within the outsider's capacity or responsibility to do anything about these conditions. If we care to help, all we can do is try to understand, accept people as they are and try to make life just a little easier for them.

That is what this book is all about. We return to Halfer and his dictum 'Them is people.'